No Drink for Me

A Candid Story of Addiction and
Journey of Self-Discovery

Lisa Peacock

mcgeary media

McGeary Media 07967 023083

I wish to dedicate this book to anyone who has ever struggled with addiction.

One day at a time...

Better days are coming.

Copyright © 2024 by Lisa Peacock

All rights reserved.

No portion of this book may be reproduced in any form without written permission from the publisher or author, except as permitted by United Kingdom copyright law.

Contents

1.	Party Girl	1
2.	Class As and Transit Vans	14
3.	Mammy's Boy	21
4.	Turning the Corner	32
5.	Confronting the Truth	46
6.	Welcome to Booze Club	58
7.	Fizzy Pop in a Fancy Bottle	79
8.	The Keys to the Chocolate Factory	90
9.	Shake a Tail Feather	96
10.	Cold Turkey	101
11.	Learning to Fly	110
12.	The Road to Recovery	118
13.	Mourning the Benders	125
14.	A Journey of Firsts	129
15.	A Stubborn Standoff	135
16.	Christmas without the Spirit	145

17.	New Year, New Job	152
18.	Back in the Rat Race	158
19.	Crete expectations	165
20.	Making the Connection	170
21.	Seizing my Second Chance	178
22.	Jesus Loves You!	183
23.	Ticked off	189
24.	A Fish out Of Water	193
25.	Dropping a Clanger	198
26.	Charlie's Angel	205
27.	The Final Countdown	216
28.	How the Saints Stole My Soberversary	222
29.	The Eagle has Landed	228

Chapter One

Party Girl

I'll get straight to the point. There is no dramatic story, no major incident in my life, that made me say, 'I'm going to start drinking every night.' I have nobody to blame except myself for not seeing how serious my problem was earlier, or for having enough self-control to know when enough was enough. I just like a drink—that's it. Party Lisa. You can depend on me for a wild night. The one thing I'm good at is partying. Fancy a bevvy? You know who to call. I should have had flyers printed. Home is just a place to crash in between binges. I'm the life and soul of the party. Or at least, I thought I was.

Throughout my formative years, nothing else mattered. Not education, career, driving, saving or getting onto the property ladder. I just lived for the weekend. Often, I didn't even wait for the weekend. I didn't care about how much my drinking cost me, including most of my relationships. The party lights and the lure of alcohol blinded me. Why is that? Why am I different? Why can't I stop?

I can't remember exactly how old I was when I had my first drink, but I was younger than ten. Each year we visited Cayton Bay Holiday Park in Scarborough—imagine a low-budget Butlin's. I have such fond memories of these times with my family. Winkle picking at the beach, riding tandem bikes and a singalong at the club every evening. We stayed in a static caravan, and it was always cold at night. I am the only girl, with two older brothers, Darren and Stephen, and a younger brother, Sean. Darren and Stephen could go off and play by themselves, but Sean and I had to stay where Mam and Dad could see us.

I vividly remember sitting on Dad's knee one night in the social club. I was wearing a light-coloured dress. There was a band on stage, and people were singing and dancing. The grown-ups on our table—Mam, Dad, my aunties, Rose and Vera, and uncles, Griff and Danny—were having such fun. There was a party atmosphere, everyone on holiday and feeling loose. I watched Dad lift his glass and drink brown liquid with a fluffy white top. All the other adults had one too. The men had big glasses and the ladies had much smaller ones. I wanted one too, so I pestered Dad for a sip until he finally gave in. I knew it was slightly naughty—Mam said it was mucky beer and I wouldn't like it. But I still wanted a taste. The huge pint glass was too big for my little hands and Dad had to hold its weight. And I took that first sip. At first I liked it, but then came the bitter taste in the back of my throat. I pulled a face and everyone laughed. But once the taste had gone, I wanted another sip just to be sure.

'All right,' said Dad. 'But just one more...'

This time I enjoyed the feeling it gave me. I giggled and felt like one of the adults. From that night on, I always pestered the grown-ups for a sip. I suppose they thought a sip couldn't do any harm. They weren't to know I was taking a sip from every adult in the room.

Back at home in Stockton, Mam and Dad went out to the Buffs Social Club. My parents, aunties and uncles loved a good party, and so did us kids, because we got to stay up late and tipsy visitors would sneak us pocket money. Men drank beer and women drank wine. Wine quickly became my favourite too. I couldn't wait to be a grown-up lady, drinking wine from my own glass. I remember playing dolls with one woman, and she let me sip her wine, sweet liquid poured from a brown bottle with a smiling nun on the front. Drinking was what adults did to have fun. I didn't see any in the house during the week, but at the weekends, well, everything seemed to come alive. Anyone who was drinking was having such a good time, laughing and dancing around.

As the only girl in the family, they expected me to be prim and cute. But I just wasn't like that. Dad called me 'Calamity Jane'. I wanted to be grown up like my big brothers, so I tried to impress them and be tough like they were. We got up to no good, climbing into a sleeping bag and sliding down the stairs on the toy box lid, scrambling onto the garage roof, rolling Dad's van down the hill with the handbrake off and playing knock-door-run. They were the Three Musketeers and I was Calamity Jane. When they challenged me with a dare, I was happy to oblige and prove how brave I was—I wasn't just a stupid girl. Once, they dared me to drink some beer from Uncle Danny's home brew, which he kept in a barrel under the stairs. The hardest thing was opening the tap quickly enough that it didn't make a noise. We sat Sean with the grown-ups and Darren was in charge of closing the front room door without attracting attention. Stephen's job was to watch me and make sure I did it and didn't chicken out. I felt a nervous knot in my tummy, but I was also excited. I twisted the tap and the beer spurted out into my face, but I quickly aimed some into my mouth and showed Stephen before closing the tap again. We all fell about the kitchen floor laughing, my brothers holding their tummies and me with my sticky-beer face. We had got away with it. After this, we loved visiting Aunty Vera's house, and drinking beer straight from the tap became a regular trick. Is this where it all began? My weakness for booze?

Even from an early age I was defiant. I was nine when a teacher accused me of scratching a desk with a needle. I wasn't guilty, but she didn't believe me, and wouldn't let the subject go. Who did she think she was, accusing me? I wasn't having that. I stood up and walked casually out through the playground and made my way home.

When I was eleven, I went to senior school and started experimenting with alcohol. I met lots of new friends in my new school and we saved our pocket money and hung around outside shops, asking strangers to buy us alcohol to drink on sleepovers or in the park. My pals and I were careful not to get too drunk. We kept the bedroom windows open so the fumes wouldn't give us away. Slowly but surely, drinking crept in unnoticed and became the dominant feature of my life. I wished the days away, waiting impatiently for the weekend. Soon I was drinking in parks with kids from other schools. Most were older than me and I upped my drinking game to impress them. I didn't want them thinking I was less grown-up than they were. I vaguely recall staggering around a school field clinging on to a Jack Daniel's bottle.

I bunked off school whenever I could. Living in a house without rules, I hated being told what to do by my teachers. I was a free spirit, unwilling to be tamed. Although I hated school, I loved art, drama, PE and maths, and would often tailor my day around these subjects, nicking off for the start of the day and slipping back in for the lessons I liked. With four kids to feed and clothe, Mam made sure we had everything we needed by holding down three part-time jobs. One was as a cleaner in the Tall Trees hotel and nightclub in leafy Yarm. She insisted on taking me to work with her early in the morning, before school started. I would skip into the empty nightclub with an empty school bag, jumping around and waving to the receptionist. When Mam's shift was over I moved more slowly, making sure the chink of the bottles and cans I had lifted from the unguarded shelves wouldn't give me away. Mam drove me to the school gate, but I rarely went in. After she dropped me off I walked straight through the grounds to the back entrance and then to the local shop for a packet of ten fags and then waited on the corner near my friend's house. As soon as her mam had gone to work I walked into her house with my swag, cans of warm Red Stripe and bottles of sweet-tasting Cherry B and Castaway. We watched Madonna's Blonde Ambition tour over and over, learning all the dance moves and being careful not to drink too much—just a gentle buzz before heading off to the lessons we could endure.

We saved up our dinner money to buy more fags and drink at the weekend. By the time I was twelve I was already going to nightclubs, borrowing paper driving licences from friends' older sisters to get past the bouncers. Once, the police raided the club to check for ID, and we hid, stifling giggles in the toilet cubicle until the coast was clear.

I was living the life, and I didn't have a care in the world. My focus was on the weekend and I cared little about what happened at school during the week. I was a bright kid but had zero interest in learning. It just wasn't a priority. Life as a real adult seemed so far away. My abiding memory of my thirteenth birthday is my friends closing my garden gate on their way to the park while I laid on the stone patio vomiting. I was too drunk on super-strength Diamond White cider to follow them. The paving slabs were cool and welcoming to my hot-flushed face. I should have recognised the warning signs back then, but I was just an out-of-control child. Thirteen sounds young, doesn't it? But where we lived, it was normal. I hung around with older girls who got up to much worse. I sometimes still felt self-conscious, as they were older and seemed wiser. Compared to them, I was just a kid, naive and flat-chested. I didn't feel as pretty as the others. Something was missing. Drink made me complete though. It gave me the confidence I lacked. Who cared if I wasn't as good-looking as them? My outgoing, booze-fueled personality made up for it. My school friends were noticing boys and acted all giddy when they were around. The talk was all about makeup, hair and clothes. I was too mature for them. My only topic of conversation was drinking and partying. I had no interest in boys.

I got to know people at the Tall Trees when I tagged along with Mam, and after a while they offered me my first job. I washed dishes and cleaning tables in the restaurant kitchen. Sometimes they even asked me to babysit for the guests. I was just a kid myself, and not a very responsible one, and there I was looking after other children. But hey, it was 1991! I made sure I washed up when I worked there on Sundays, which meant I could polish off the dregs of expensive wine dotted around the kitchen, which the previous night's patrons had left behind. I was so drunk by the time my shift ended at five o'clock that I was still worse for wear at school on Monday.

By the age of fourteen I was visiting nightclubs and bars regularly. I loved the excitement of trying our luck at different venues—will they let us in or won't they? The buzz of doing something naughty appealed to me. I craved excitement and drama. Rules were made to be broken and I was born to break them. Buying new clothes to look older than I was became expensive. And because I could gulp them down so quickly, I needed more cash for drinks as well. Some Fridays I didn't have enough money for nightclubs and slummed it at the youth club, smuggling in neat Martini to lace the icy, bright blue Slush Puppies they sold.

Looking back, it's hard to understand how I didn't know something was seriously wrong. I suppose I couldn't see the wood for the trees. Just like in an abusive relationship, I loved alcohol and I thought alcohol loved me. I wasn't fussy about where I drank. One favourite trick was walking Lucy, our collie-cross rescue dog, to the bookies, betting on a few greyhound races and then spending any winnings on a few pints in the nearest pub. Greyhounds and old men's pubs might not be typical activities for a young lady, but I was far from your average schoolgirl! Our other dog, Toby, was a bad-tempered Yorkshire terrier. We tried our best to train him, but he only became more and more vicious, and we had no choice but to give him up. But the whole family missed him and the kennels called us asking if we could have him back and we said we would. When we arrived, Toby was sharing a kennel with eleven-month-old Lucy and she seemed to calm him. So we left the kennels that day with both of them.

Booze became my pied piper, taking me down dark streets and into dangerous places with dangerous people, but I followed like a loyal puppy. It had burrowed deep inside my brain, a constant voice wherever I went, telling me everything would be fine if we just stayed together. Everything would work out as long as I stayed faithful. And I did. Once I learned to love drink I couldn't unlearn it, couldn't get it out of my mind, couldn't turn off the adoration. I looked for bigger and better thrills. Never mind smoking cannabis as a gateway drug—I went straight for gold. I was in a nightclub with my best friend, Gemma. (That's not her real name, but she's now a social worker—her role in my story might not look great on her CV.) She was as wild as me but had more rules at home, so she often slept over at my house where we could get away with more. Other times I told my parents I was sleeping at hers and she told her mam she was sleeping at mine, and we stayed out all night. On this particular night, a male acquaintance gave us a small square paper tab of acid. I was thrilled. We rushed straight to the ladies' toilets and locked ourselves in a cubicle. Then I held the prize in my palm, as though fearful it would explode if I dropped it. We glanced nervously at each other and giggled, two fourteen-year-old kids about to swallow class A drugs. After a brief exchange about how dangerous taking acid could be, we egged each other on. I tore the tab in half with my teeth and we each took our share. That night changed me forever. I stepped into another universe where I could lose myself, a parallel world with no school and no rules. We returned to the dance floor and huddled together for hours, laughing wildly at the flashing of the disco lights.

At school on Monday morning I felt more detached from my school friends than ever. I couldn't wait until the next weekend to try something else. Then I heard whispers about a drug called ecstasy. Some of the older boys we hung around with were going to a party at the weekend where everyone would be taking it, and I wanted in. One lad was already driving, and he offered to take me. When the big night came, I squashed into his already full Vauxhall Cavalier and drove to an old barn in the middle of a field. I looked around and saw abandoned cars strewn all over the place, with people dancing and swaying everywhere—I had arrived at my first illegal rave. There was so much energy and people were so friendly, hugging me and making me dance with them. Full of confidence, and in the party mood after drinking vodka in the car, I knew I belonged here. We soon met a dealer and I handed over ten whole pounds for an ecstasy tablet, a considerable amount in those days—I had to wash a lot of pots to earn that. I swallowed the drug down almost immediately, along with a gulp of my vodka. It rapidly took effect and within forty minutes I felt magical, pure euphoria and happiness swirling all around me, my body free and uninhibited. Boy, did I dance. I covered every inch of that field until the sun rose.

After that, I wanted more. I spent weekends nightclubbing and then searching for the next rave to keep the happy feelings coming. Drugs were becoming a regular feature in my life, but drinking was still my favourite game. I didn't have a care in the world and life couldn't have been better. But things were about to take a turn for the worse. My parents shocked me by announcing we were moving house. Not just to another town but to bloody Leicestershire, more than 100 miles away. One by one, Teesside's many iron foundries were closing down, and Dad had lost his job as a fettler. With four kids to look after and nothing available in the area, he had to go where the work was.

Even with Mam doing three cleaning jobs, Dad being jobless was out of the question. I felt devastated. I had just found myself, and now I had to say goodbye to everything I knew and loved.

I hated everything about the Midlands. I was now fifteen and had gone from being surrounded by friends and invited to every party to obscurity, the unknown new kid in town. People talked funny and would call me duck. 'Duck'? Grow up! It's 'pet' up north! I despised my new school. Mam walked me to the bus stop and waited until she saw me get on. But nothing had changed. At the other end I just walked into town, spending some of my days in a church, flicking through an Argos catalogue and trying to keep warm. When the sun shone, I sat on a bench and fed chips to the pigeons. I longed to be back home. I made a few friends, but it just wasn't the same. Although they were my age, they were still drinking in parks. For me, that was all in the past. I was too grown-up now. After a few weeks, I finally persuaded them to brave a pub. Nightclubs would have to wait, baby steps would do for now. Besides, the nearest nightclub was twenty miles away in Leicester. We got the bus to Market Harborough, where our school was, and headed towards The Talbot. My new friends were nervous they wouldn't get in, so I marched to the front, full of confidence. I had lied about my age many times. This was a doddle and I greeted the doormen in my broad northern accent.

'Evening lads!'

I even got a cheeky wink as they opened the door for me. I'm not interested guys, I'm only here for the cider. If they only knew I wasn't even sixteen. The bar had sawdust on the floor and was thick with the smell of dope as Pink Floyd's *Comfortably Numb* played on the jukebox. The pub had a far older crowd and a slower pace than I was used to, but I was out, I was breaking rules, and I had a pint of cider in my hand. After a couple of hours we ran out of money, having spent every penny we had on booze. With no bus fare, I convinced the others we would be perfectly safe hitchhiking home. Four tipsy fifteen-year-old schoolgirls in a stranger's car. What could possibly go wrong? We'll never know. A couple of hundred yards down the road the police picked us up. The other girls started crying, terrified about what their parents would say. I was over the moon—we got a free lift home.

As soon as their parents released the other girls from being grounded, I once again talked them around to my way of thinking. I could be very persuasive. This time we hitched a lift into Leicester and the girls experienced the rowdy and exciting world of a nightclub for the first time. I loved meeting new people and pretending I was much older than I was, and they always believed me. I soon realised the city had a much better nightlife to offer than my northern hometown and I relished the extra attention that came my way as my Teesside accent made me stand out. Life was free. I was on a permanent holiday and I didn't take anything seriously. I didn't have to.

Soon I found work in a local restaurant, just washing up and helping serve food, but even better than the money I earned was how the job opened up my party life. I got to go out more and to bigger and better clubs. My circle of friends widened, and some older lads introduced me to the underground rave scene and showed me where to score drugs. I experimented with whatever I could get my hands on—LSD, MDMA, cocaine and amphetamines. While my friends were spending Friday nights revising for their GCSEs, I was queuing up for Miss Moneypenny's in Birmingham. One night a well-known DJ invited us into a VIP suite where I drank champagne straight from the bottle—if only they knew I was still at school! It gave me such a kick to be a rebel. I couldn't wait to leave school and find a proper job.

When I finally left, of course, I had no qualifications. I found full-time work packing shoes in a factory. It was mindless drudgery, but I loved it. I spent my time adding up my wages in my head and daydreaming about what I would spend it on—usually clothes, alcohol, drugs and clubbing. Certainly not saving, a pension or investing. I didn't give a second thought to my future. Every Friday I darted off to the pub with my little brown envelope and handed a large portion of my earnings over to the landlord. It was a tradition, as far as I was concerned. It's what I watched everyone else do and so I did it too. I was so obsessed with going to the pub that I often missed the driving lessons I'd booked. Drink was more important anyway.

Chapter Two

Class As and Transit Vans

By the time I was seventeen I wanted to drink every night, even on the rare evenings I stayed in. My body told me to. I was alcohol dependent. It could be tricky getting served in some shops, but I could always rely on one off-licence in town, and when the cravings got too much I would walk down and pick up a bottle of cheap La Mancha white wine. I finished work at 1pm on Friday and headed to the aptly named Shambles pub with my wage packet. One time, at around 10pm, one of the older lads mentioned he was going to a club called Wobble in Birmingham. He told me the entire building shook with the beat of the music and the DJ's decks had to be suspended from chains to counterbalance the movement. I had already been drinking for around nine hours, but I wanted in on this trip, so I rushed home to change into something fashionably skimpy. I drank another bottle of cider on the journey and arrived at the club with a bra full of ecstasy tablets. My recollection of what went on inside the venue is hazy. I remember laughing and joking with the doormen, then looking for the famous hanging decks and struggling to find them. The thud of the music running through my body paired with the rush of the MDMA had me in a spin, fumbling along mirrored walls. I must have entered blackout after that, as I can't remember anything else until we were back at my friend's house. I was sitting on a sofa snorting cocaine with a glass of cider in hand. It was nearly ten in the morning, still an hour to kill before the pubs opened at eleven. We spent the rest of Saturday drinking pints and feeding pound coins into the jukebox to play our favourite tunes. I still hadn't slept, but when Gaz, one of the regular pub crowd, proposed a trip to the Rise rave night at the Leadmill club in Sheffield, I was up for it again. He had just bought a Ford Transit van and could fit a few people in the back, he said. I went home and grabbed a bag of clothes and makeup and then met Gaz in a car park. When he opened the back doors, a bolted-down three-seater sofa was waiting for us—we would travel in style! The van was an old model and one of the back windows was missing, so Gaz had carefully Clingfilmed the missing square. We arrived at a service station just outside Sheffield so we could all get changed in the toilets. It must have looked like a scene from Stars in Your Eyes when the back doors opened, with smoke billowing out into the cold night air—'Tonight Matthew, I will mostly be stoned…' I remember the club not being as good as we expected and we headed home, stopping off at an off-licence for more supplies—we had a house party to cater for. As usual, we sat in the front room lazing on sofas, listening to music and passing the spliffs around before going to another pub to brace ourselves for Monday morning. By now I was shaking like a shitting dog, the drink, drugs and lack of sleep taking its toll on me. I needed a drink to pull round. The scene at work on the Monday was not pretty. I was still coming down and mega anxious unable to eat a thing, and yet I couldn't wait to do it all again. I cringe when I think back. I didn't just push the party boundaries, but I abused my body and put my life at risk. Getting stoned in the back of a bloody Tranny van, taking drugs and drinking to blackout? I'm lucky I'm still alive to tell the tale.

When Dad lost his job in the foundry, my parents decided we would move back to Teesside. Once again, I felt devastated. I had only just found my feet in Leicester. I loved my new life and had to be dragged home kicking and screaming. When I got there I was also jobless, which meant I didn't know where my next drink was coming from. A trip to a pawn shop bridged the gap until I found work, and I sold everything of any worth, jewellery, stereo and DVDs. After a few weeks I got a job in Visage nightclub in Stockton, lying about my age and giving a fake National Insurance number. I worked on the front desk taking the admission money. Everyone was polite on the way in, playful, fun and flirty. But it was a different story on the way out. The girls often staggered out on their high heels, makeup smudged and hair out of place. The lads, meanwhile, struggled to stand up as they slurred chat-up lines in a last-ditch attempt to persuade someone into going home with them. Some asked for my number, and they didn't always take it well when I gently let them down. One became abusive.

'Who do you think you are, you slag!'

Thankfully, the doormen had taken me under their wing and his face dropped as they came over and shoved him out onto the street.

As soon as the doors shut each Saturday night we were closed until the following weekend. That meant we had to empty the drink that was left in the lines to prevent it from going stale. I made sure I syphoned off the cider. Even at my tender age, I could out-drink all the burly security staff in our after-hours sessions.

The 1990s ushered in the era of the ladette. It felt like equality. I could smoke and drink as much as any bloke could. At gigs and parties I swilled pint after pint, just like one of the lads. I wanted a boyfriend and to be loved, but tear-arsing around town acting drunk and lairy only earned me a reputation for being a good-time girl. I knew how to attract attention, but the wrong kind of attention. Men took advantage of me, and I took advantage of them, making sure they bought me drinks.

I was sometimes so skint and desperate I went 'minesweeping'. A friend and I got dressed up and headed into town with no money. We didn't need it. We just walked around busy bars and clubs picking other people's drinks up when they went to the loo or just weren't paying attention. We usually found some boys to buy us drinks before too long. Lads working in

Middlesbrough from outside the area were easy targets. It was a dangerous game, but I loved to play. Safety was the last thing on my mind when I wanted a drink.

Given a choice, drink always came before my health. When Toby—aka 'Mam's mad dog'—bit me again, one of the two puncture wounds in my leg was so deep I had to go to hospital. To my horror, the doctors kept me in and put me on an intravenous drip to pump antibiotics into my bloodstream. My first thought was how was I going to drink? Surely I could manage a few nights without? They took me to a small ward where three lovely elderly ladies occupied the other three beds. They cooed around me and one asked how big the dog that bit me was. I blushed as I admitted it was a tiny Yorkshire Terrier!

I was allowed to roam the hospital, pulling a stand with a hanging bag of medication on it. Classy look. In the day room I got chatting to a guy called Alan, who had been in hospital for several weeks after jumping off a roof and shattering his legs. He ignored me when I asked what kind of idiot would jump off such a high roof! We struck up a bond though, and I told him I could murder a drink.

'There's an off-licence just over the road,' he said.

When I pointed out that they wouldn't let me leave the hospital towing a drip, he spun around in his wheelchair.

'Your wish is my command,' he said.

I handed over some money and he sped off down the corridor, shouting back to the nurses that he was going out for a pizza.

Fifteen minutes later he did indeed return with a pizza, a cheesy smokescreen to cover the three-litre box of wine he was hiding for me. We sat in the dayroom eating pizza and watching Saturday night TV, *Gladiators*, *Blind Date* and *Stars in Their Eyes*, with my glass of wine in one hand and a drip in the other.

I muddled through the next few years, doing different jobs that I usually lost soon afterwards for turning up late or being too hungover to be of use to anyone. I also left a string of meaningless relationships in my wake. I still longed to feel loved, but drinking pint after pint every night didn't make me girlfriend material. I was more like one of the lads.

By the time I was twenty-one I worked in an amusement arcade by day, still pubbing it every night. As soon as my shift finished I headed straight to the bar by myself. I usually sat with the old boys, who taught me to play darts until I was better than most of them. Nearly every day someone would ask what a young lass like me was doing in a dingy old pub on my own. I didn't have an answer, except that I loved it. Standing at the bar and being handed a cool pint of cider just seemed the natural thing to do after a hard day at work. That first, refreshing sip washed away the grime of the day and I felt my shoulders relax as the liquid ran down my throat. I joined in the cards and dominoes games, laughing and joking, without a worry in the world. I spent whatever I had in my pocket, choosing to buy one last pint rather than pay for a taxi, putting drink before my own safety again. And then I would wobble home alone.

I was also stealing. It's not something I would deliberately do, but when I blacked out through too much drink I became a different person. I woke up to find all sorts of things in my home—traffic cones, garden gnomes and bottles of milk that had been left out on householders' doorsteps. One morning I opened my eyes and felt something heavy on my chest. I lifted the bed covers off to find a full set of wheel trims in bed with me. Weirdly, they were a perfect fit for my mam's blue Ford Escort. Well, I had no way of finding their rightful owner, so I might as well use them, right?

Chapter Three

Mammy's Boy

By the age of twenty-three, I had been taken over by alcohol. I knew I had a problem and I wanted to stop. I tried hard to have more self-control, promising myself I would only drink at the weekend, but giving in and finding myself in the pub again by Tuesday. On the rare occasions when I stayed in, I promised myself I'd only drink the one bottle of wine, but I knew I'd open a second. I constantly let myself down. I just couldn't do it. Drink was the only thing I needed and soon I didn't recognise myself at all. Finally, I looked for outside help, telling my doctor that I felt so low I didn't want to live anymore. I had nothing to live for. Drinking dominated my life. She arranged for me to see a counsellor and I arrived for the first session, planning what I was going to say. But as soon as I sat down I started sobbing, and I cried so much I never had time to talk about my problems. All I managed to get out was how much I wanted to stop drinking.

My body also started showing the effects of the poison I consumed every day. That's why I thought nothing of it when I took a funny turn at work just after my lunch break, feeling shaky and sick. The same thing happened the next day, and again the day after that. Finally, the penny dropped. I ran to the chemist and bought a pregnancy test and took it to the staff toilets, where the result confirmed why I felt out of sorts. I had been seeing a guy I had worked with in my previous job. I was the other woman, of course. Nobody would have committed to a party girl like me. I had never even considered having children. In fact I never looked beyond the following day. I had nothing to look forward to anyway. Bringing a baby into a life as grim as mine would have been madness. But the decision to keep the new life growing inside me was an easy one. I felt a mix of emotions, shocked, terrified, but strangely happy. When I visited my counsellor again the next week, I didn't cry at all and I announced I wouldn't be seeing her again. I was having a baby. I stopped drinking from the second I saw those two positive lines.

Not drinking throughout my pregnancy was easy, because it wasn't about me any more. I was giving up for someone else, an innocent and vulnerable baby who couldn't protect themselves. Luckily, I sailed through the pregnancy with no physical health issues. But devastating bouts of anxiety plagued me. I constantly worried something would go wrong. Every night I tried to imagine my baby's face: would it be a boy or a girl? I had names for both outcomes, Cara for a girl and Jimi for a boy. Four weeks before my due date, the midwife raised concerns about the size of my baby. A scan was arranged and the jolly sonographer told me the baby I was expecting would weigh at least eleven pounds. I told the baby's father, who informed me, to my horror, that he had weighed thirteen pounds at birth.

I was due to be induced at noon on delivery day. I can tell you, waiting to give birth to an eleven-pound baby is pretty scary. The face staring back at me from the mirror was a sickly shade of green. No way was I going to pass anything other than a baby in that birthing room, and the six slices of brown toast I ate that morning did the trick. At 11.29pm on Wednesday March 12th 2003, my little boy entered the world. Baby Jimi. People had laughed at me and said Jimi was old-fashioned, but the second I saw my baby I knew the name belonged to him. He was perfect, with huge, saucer-like eyes, perfect lips and a shock of thick, brown hair that was so unusual that nurses from different departments around the hospital visited to meet the baby with the hair.

You think you have loved before, but nothing compares to a mother's love for a child. I couldn't wait to get him home. But once I arrived there, after the euphoria of Jimi's arrival, it hit me just how hard my life would be. I didn't have the first idea of how to look after a baby. I had read the books and been to the classes, but actually doing it was a different prospect.

Jimi's dad continued to be a feature in my life. The thought of being a father did not put him off, and within a few weeks of Jimi being born, we moved in together. This was another enormous shock to my system. I had only ever lived with my parents—I didn't even make my own bed. What's more, I loved Jimi so much. He was my new life, but I also felt I was losing the old Lisa and the wild existence I had led. But we soon settled into a routine and life felt good again. I shed the extra pounds I had put on and went back to work part-time at the amusement arcade. The more confident I grew, however, the more my partner's behaviour changed. He became jealous and controlling, often questioning what I was wearing, where I was going and who I was going with. I suppose my party reputation had caught up with me. He didn't want me going back to the life I was living when we met. After eighteen months of constantly checking over my shoulder, I'd had enough. But I had to summon all my strength to tell him to leave, and I felt a deep sense of guilt for chasing little Jimi's dad away.

After two weeks of blazing rows, he finally left. From now on, me and Jimi were on our own. Although I knew it would be difficult bringing a child up without his father's help, I also felt enormous relief. I could do what I wanted. I started going out with friends again and even joined a theatre group. Jimi was my parents' only grandchild and my family gave me so much support. They were more than happy to spend time with him, and I was happy to take advantage of their kindness. But as my confidence returned, my faithful old friend sneaked back into my life. After Jimi went off to sleep, the familiar struggle began. It started with a glass of wine each night, just to wash away the day of potty training and singing the alphabet and to get me through to the weekend, when I could finally let my hair down again. My weekends were so wild that by Monday I was so low that I needed more drink just to feel normal. In the blink of an eye I was drinking a bottle of wine every night to blot out the loneliness and the woes of being a single mother. Being both mum and dad would never be easy, breadwinner and homemaker, blending the need to be gentle and nurturing while also making sure Jimi was strong and brave enough to face the outside world. Alcohol had been my constant companion for so long, and soon we were back together as if Jimi had never happened. And together, we spiralled back into a vicious cycle of hopelessness and depression. It's funny how I never thought drinking was a factor in my low mood.

Despite my illness, I still cared for Jimi as well as I could. I helped him practise his reading, taught him about the planets and visited the park to kick up the piles of autumn leaves. We made indoor tents and enjoyed picnics on the carpet. But when Jimi's little legs tired and he disappeared off to bed, it was grown-up time. I hated myself for drinking. So if I hated myself, why did I keep doing it? Such thoughts swirled around my head until the alcohol smothered them and numbed any negative emotions. But as soon as I awoke for the school run, the self-loathing kicked in again.

I got myself into such a state that I slowly retreated from society. My anxiety was so bad I couldn't even leave the house. My family, and especially my parents, were a tremendous help. I couldn't have looked after Jimi without them. But even now, a prisoner in my home, the link between alcohol and my mental health never occurred to me and I continued to drink heavily. I tried to get help from my GP, but they said they couldn't support me because I drank too much—but I drank too much because I had mental health issues. The two conditions went hand in hand, and I couldn't turn one off. In desperation I found a private therapist who could help me. I had to use savings I had put aside for our summer holiday, but I figured if I got better I could return to work and pick up extra shifts to pay the money back. It took twelve weeks and several false starts before I finally returned to work at the arcade, and to some kind of normality. But although I could function at a basic level, I continued drinking every night.

I stumbled through life as the years went by, trying to balance the role of a single mum with my drinking, and just to say making it through each day, despite the iron grip alcohol had on me. Around about the time Jimi started senior school, we also moved house. Both events presented an opportunity to make a fresh start and put my troubled past behind me. I even felt well enough to dip my toe into the online dating scene. That's when I met Danny. Seven years younger than me, Danny's dark hair and brown eyes reflected his Italian ancestry. From our very first date, he treated me like a princess. I was used to being just one of the lads in the pub crowd, but Danny opened doors, brought me flowers and whisked me off for weekends away. In fact, he seemed too good to be true. I was on the back foot and kept waiting for the catch. No one had ever made me feel this special. But although Danny clearly saw something loveable in me, I didn't feel the same way. I wasn't good enough for him, I told myself, and I couldn't understand why he wanted to be with me. I knew it would all go wrong. Like every other man, he would hurt me and walk away. But just eight weeks after that first date, Danny gave me a moment I will never forget, and for all the right reasons. Jimi and I were on holiday in Malaga with my parents and Danny had caught a later flight out to join us. After a lovely day visiting an aquarium, he walked me down to the beach and presented me with a bottle of champagne and a Milka chocolate bar. That's when he said he had fallen in love with me. I can remember the sheer joy welling up inside when I heard these words. But nothing was just about me any more. I told Danny I loved him as well, but there wasn't just me to love. There was Jimi too. Danny promised to take care of both of us. Even though I now had everything I had ever wanted in my life, an amazing child and a handsome man by my side, I continued to drink. As much as I loved Danny and Jimi, I loved alcohol, too. And I still wasn't ready to allow myself to be happy. My self-esteem had taken such a battering over the years and the niggling feeling I didn't deserve him refused to go away. It was only a year later, when we moved in together, that Danny realised the extent of my drinking. He didn't mention it—he didn't need to. I could see the shock and horror on his face as I drained a second bottle of wine on an ordinary weekday night. I knew I was risking everything, but I needed booze in my life just as much as I needed Danny. But the guilt about what I was doing and the terrifying prospect of losing my best and perhaps my only chance of finding true happiness eventually prompted me to take action. I had heard of a local addiction support group called Change Grow Live (CGL), and I got in touch to arrange an appointment. I had to keep my cry for help silent—I couldn't risk Danny finding out how serious my problem was because I was convinced he would leave me when he realised I was too damaged to be loved. I had been dumped in almost every relationship I have ever been in, tossed aside for someone better. If Danny found out, he was sure to find a stronger girl without the baggage I dragged along with me. I was mortified to have got into such a mess. Going to counselling would be my secret affair. This was my problem and I had to sort it myself. I made every telephone call during work time and arranged cloak and dagger face-to-face appointments. I would have made an excellent secret agent, creeping around in my hoody and even shredding car park tickets to destroy the evidence. I had no intention of giving up drinking. I just wanted some sort of control. Maybe only drinking at weekends.

The sessions lasted six weeks. At first my drinking slowed down, but soon my weekends included Mondays, then I'd have a drink on Wednesday—you know, just to break the week up. Before long I was drinking every night again. I hated myself. Nobody else cared or even noticed the severity of my problem. Guilt and anger consumed me. I was desperate to be a different person, a better mother, a daughter to be proud of, a caring sister and a loving partner to Danny. I knew that woman was somewhere within me. She occasionally emerged, before being pushed back into her place by my wilder side, who was always the one in charge. You deserve a drink. It's no big deal. Everyone does it.

With Danny now in the house, relieving my cravings was more challenging. I'm a people-pleaser by nature and I now had two people in my life to please, and sometimes I felt torn in two. Jimi was a teenager and his hormones were everywhere. The atmosphere in the house became tense and angry, with explosive rows an everyday occurrence. My solution? Drink more, of course. But being hungover, tired and therefore short-tempered made bringing up a temperamental teenager even more challenging. We argued most mornings and I didn't have the patience to deal with his tantrums. I would snap back at him and then cry on the drive to work and feel guilty all day. I tried to make it up by preparing Jimi's favourite meal, lasagne, for him to come home to, and then opened a bottle of wine, repeating the cycle all over again. But my drinking only fuelled the next battle.

When Jimi left school, I decided we would go travelling. The plan was for Danny, Jimi and I to drive off into the sunset in an old Land Rover we had fitted out specially for the trip of a lifetime. Sadly, that's not quite how the story unfolded. Jimi didn't want to come. I can understand why. He was reluctant to leave his friends and his hometown, and the prospect of spending months in a tiny space with us can't have helped, all sleeping together in a dusty old truck. I tried telling him what an incredible opportunity he had to see the world at such a young age, but Jimi had decided. I now had a choice. Should I stay in my humdrum life or follow my dream? I had always planned to travel when I reached my forties and after weeks of mental torture, I finally decided I needed to go. Jimi would be safe and well looked after with his grandparents, and I would only be away for around eighteen months. A few friends supported my decision, but most judged me, making me feel like I was abandoning my son.

'Oh, I couldn't leave my son behind like that,' one said. Nobody is asking you to, I thought. I don't tell people how to run their lives, so why did people feel they could tell me how to run mine? I wasn't leaving him with a murderer. He would be with close relatives who loved him very much. We found Jimi a place studying electrical engineering at college and I started making preparations for our adventure.

Saying goodbye and driving away from my little boy was one of the hardest things I have ever done. I was eaten up by guilt and cried every day for a long time. However, there was always one confidante I could always rely on to soothe the pain and make me feel human—booze. Not only was there an endless supply, but it was dirt cheap. And after all, I was on holiday, wasn't I? I flitted around Europe drinking whatever I could get my hands on—raki, limoncello, vodka, grappa and many other delights on offer. Don't you know it's rude to turn down a shot? I even camped in vineyards—aka Blackout City. That was what I called the regular occasions, in fact more nights than not, when I drank so much I couldn't remember what I'd done the night before. Travelling gave me a green light to party every night and drink more than ever. I didn't even have the prospect of getting up for work the next morning to tame me.

Chapter Four

Turning the Corner

It took a devastating pandemic to bring me crashing back down to earth with a shattering bump. In the summer of 2020, with the world closed down to deal with the threat of Covid, we had no choice but to return to the UK. Coming home was a sharp shock to the system. I went from wearing flip-flops without a care in the world to the gritty reality of work and life back on Teesside. But it was the best thing that could have happened to me. I finally realised just how bad my drink problem had become. I wasn't drinking for fun any more, I was drinking just to feel normal.

A friend bought me a birthday gift and I unwrapped the paper to reveal a beautiful crystal bottle stopper. I looked at it, then looked at her and we both burst out laughing.

'I have no idea why I bought that,' she said. 'You'll never use it!'

I never left wine in the bottle for the next day, so why would I need a stopper?

Everybody saw the fun side of me, the wild, carefree, confident women. Only I experienced the dark side, the turmoil within my brain. I kept it well hidden, the me who couldn't see past getting drunk every single night, and beating myself up until it was time to drink again.

One evening after work, I found myself waiting at some traffic lights. If I turned right, I went home; turn left, and I could buy alcohol. Good Lisa wanted to turn right, but Bad Lisa gave in to the cravings, snatching at the indicator so hard it almost snapped the stalk. I wanted to be normal—just one, maybe two glasses of cold white wine with my tea and then return the bottle to its shelf in the fridge. Why did I have to fill the glass all the way to the top? I'll just have a quick slurp, so it doesn't spill over. Why couldn't I stop until the bottle was gone? Why did I always open another? Why did I need to drink myself into oblivion?

I was like a buckled wheel most nights. Danny usually went to bed early, and I stayed up because I wanted to get drunk alone. Well into the early hours, when the bottles were all empty, I staggered into bed. A couple of hours later I would wake up desperate for the loo, and that was it for the night. I'd lie there, unable to sleep and worrying that I'd be hungover in the morning. Why did I get so drunk knowing I was at work the next day?

I had everything I'd ever wanted—a wonderful son who deserved better than me, and a loving partner who I had waited my entire life to meet. I had great friends and I was looking forward to the chance to travel again in the future. Apart from the mundane nine-till-five job, I was living the dream. And yet I still let drink ruin me. I can understand people who drink every day because they have nothing left to lose. But why did I do it?

Finally, the penny dropped. It was because I always have. I didn't know any different. I was an alcoholic. My parents enjoyed a social drink, their friends liked a drink and I had never experienced life without alcohol. And then as I grew up, I always hung around with older people who all drank heavily and did drugs.

I was pathetic. I had let alcohol control me; it dictated how I lived my life and everything I did. I couldn't stop and I despised myself for it. Most mornings I had a fuzzy head, felt sick and couldn't concentrate. One of my responsibilities at work involved overseeing the payroll and it's a wonder anyone ever got paid the right money. In the mornings my brain was on autopilot and I couldn't even remember processing the wages. By lunchtime I started feeling a little better. Well enough for another drink. Time to plan my next session. Which wine will I buy? What excuse will I give Danny this time? 'Oh, I've had such a bad day'; 'It's my time of the month' (always a good one); 'I have some good news'; 'Another old lady died...' Working as an administrator and receptionist in a care home, I saw this last one happen all too often. I had worked in a care home back in 2011, before I met Danny. I expected a slow, sleepy place to work where my days would be easy. It was nothing like that. Every day was frantic, and there was always something happening. Upset families to deal with, angry their parents had ended up in a care home setting. Husbands broken hearted they had to leave their wives behind as dementia took its grip on them. Dealing with death and sadness, sometimes daily. I left a care home in Middlesbrough to go travelling and on my return a year later found another home in Stockton. It's what I knew, so I went back. But death was just another reason to convince both Danny and myself I needed a drink. I would still have had one regardless, as Danny never questioned my drinking. In truth, I was only trying to fool myself. If only I had more self-control, I could have been good during the week and only drank at weekends. That's acceptable, isn't it? I'd have cracked it then. But I'd been telling myself the same thing for more than twenty years.

***

I don't know when I finally turned the corner. I suppose there should have been so many turning points. The time I was sick at work—a friend got married and when her wedding photographs arrived, we arranged a 'reveal'. They chose my house because I had a huge projector screen. I put food out and bought copious amounts of alcohol. I was already tipsy when the guests arrived. Everyone oohed and aahed at the photographs on the big screen, while I kept busy filling glasses and making cocktails. Then I remembered the bottles of champagne in the fridge and made sure everyone joined me in having a few glasses. My guests left at around midnight after what had been a lovely evening, and I closed the door behind them. I should have gone to bed, but I couldn't stop thinking about the last bottle of champagne in the fridge. I opened the door and stared at it, then closed the door. And then I opened the door, snatched the bottle and popped the cork. I was sick the minute I opened my eyes the next morning. I called my manager, Big Jim, and asked for a lift to work, then I jumped into the shower to wake myself up. The car journey was the longest two miles of my life. I had the window open and tried to act sober, then as soon as we got to work I ran to the loo to be sick again. It wasn't even nine o'clock. Jim found me and sent me home. I could see the disappointment on his face. I had let him down. I had let myself down. Yet I still drank again that night. I should have known then.

The time I was arrested should have made me realise things had gone too far. I had been thrown out of the pub for nodding off on the third day of a bender. I was standing in the street waiting for a taxi when I saw a friend arguing with another guy and I could see a scuffle was about to break out. I walked over and calmed my friend down and we were just walking away when a police van turned up. Two fresh-faced coppers got out and put the handcuffs on my mate. I asked why he was being arrested, as they could see we were walking away from the aggro. I didn't take too kindly to the young officer telling me to, 'Button it!' I started mouthing off, so the police officer sprayed me with CS gas and threw me into the back of the van. Still a little harsh if you ask me, but I suppose I should have kept my mouth shut and gone home. For weeks afterwards, whenever I ironed the shirt I had been wearing, the steam from the CS gas stung my eyes. I should have known enough was enough then.

Another time I was too hungover to take Jimi to play football. I woke up in a dreadful state that Sunday morning. I managed to get Jimi's kit ready, but I was too hungover to drive and had to call my parents to take him. I glanced at the mirror and saw a puffed up, red-faced drunk staring back at me. I would need a couple more hours to pull myself round before I could collect him. I arrived to see the other football mums cheering their little boys on from the sidelines, all looking perfect with full hair and makeup, in stark contrast to my red face as I offered Jimi an embarrassed little wave. It was far from being the first time I'd had to beg for a lift from my parents. I was regularly too hungover to drive to the weekly grocery shop. On the worst days I would send them a list of what I needed.

So many occasions that should have been lightbulb moments. The many times I blacked out and couldn't remember what I had done the night before. And even worse, the times I could remember what I had done the night before. The ones that still make me cringe.

One night I lay in the bath staring at the ceiling and imagined I was dead and in my coffin. I asked myself how I would feel about my life? Would I look back and be proud of how I lived? Did I make the most of the time I was given on this earth? The answer was no. I didn't live any more. I merely existed. I was an unhealthy, unfit, obese alcoholic. I wanted to seek adventure, climbing mountains, kayaking wild rivers and riding horses in faraway lands. I wanted to live to the fullest and be somebody who made a difference. I wanted a worthwhile career and to be respected. But instead I was drinking my life away. More than twenty years of juggling drinking and living with the anxiety it caused. Countless hours wasted in dreary pubs, handing over the money I could have spent on a comfortable three-bedroomed semi in a pleasant area.

I am proud of some of my achievements—my amazing son being the best of them—but I have also done many things I'm ashamed of. I knew I couldn't change the past, but I could at least try to transform my future. But how? Nothing seemed to work for me. I tried only having a couple of glasses each night, or just drinking on weekends. An attempt to reach out to a recovery group failed because I couldn't be honest. I even tried hypnotherapy, paying the therapist to convince me that drinking cider would make me feel nauseous. It worked for a few weeks, and then I missed a session. I drank eleven pints of cider and a bottle of wine that night, just to prove my therapist wrong. But this time felt different. I felt more desperate, pathetic and out of control than ever. Drinking no longer brought me pleasure; it became a necessity to satisfy my body's cravings and feel normal. Drink was dragging me down to a place I knew I didn't want to go. I hated myself more and more every day and began crying while I drank wine at home. I needed to get off this hideous ride and stop my life from slipping through my fingers. All I cared about was getting drunk. I even considered giving up my job so I had the freedom to drink whatever I wanted, whenever I wanted. Then I'd be a proper alcoholic. Of course, in truth I already was one. I could feel my life swirling around the plug-hole—and if I was washed down, I knew there would be no coming back.

One night I wrote this through my tears as I emptied yet another bottle...

> *It's a poison on my lips I just can't resist.*
> *It's the end of a long day, to sit and get pissed.*
> *A pop of a cork, the crack of a can,*
> *I lick my lips; this is who I am.*
> *I'm the life and soul, the soul of the party,*
> *Pissed up and lairy, mouthy and tarty.*
> *Let's have another, just one for the road,*
> *My eyes light up as I do as I'm told.*
> *I'll stop on Monday, is what I always say,*
> *But I'm drunk on Monday; I've had a bad day*

I needed to tell somebody how I was feeling, but I just couldn't face it. I felt embarrassed and ashamed. I also knew there would be no going back after I opened up and admitted how bad my problem was. I would have to do something about it. I couldn't even face Danny. Instead, I sent a text.

'I think I'm drinking too much and I'm going to find a local group to help me.'

My finger hovered over the send button before finally dispatching the message. I felt a churning in my guts. Would he stay by my side and help me face my battle? Or would he just up and leave me? He could easily find someone who didn't bring all these problems into his life and I wouldn't have blamed him if he did. I tried to focus on my work and not dwell on the time Danny was taking to respond. Finally, my phone bleeped.

'I know, love–it can't hurt to talk to someone about it. I will help you.'

My man of many words! I ran to the loo, shielding my face so my colleagues couldn't see the tears flowing. He thought I was worth fighting for. I wasn't sure, but he was. The knowledge wasn't enough to banish the negative thoughts that kept on saying, I'm not good enough. Why is he with me? My destructive inner voice didn't only speak out about my relationship with Danny. It was the same with friendships, work and family. Too many times I felt I had to work more and try harder to somehow prove myself. Drinking was the one thing I knew I excelled at. It didn't judge me or asked for anything from me. All it wanted in return was to steal my life.

After an emotional day at work, I returned home ready to face Danny. Even though we have now been together for many years, I was deeply ashamed and still terrified he would reject me. Sweat trickled down my palms as I reached for a bottle of wine to steady my nerves. The bottle was half empty by the time I heard the click of the door latch. Danny rushed over and pulled me into his arms. Exposing my vulnerability was one of the hardest things I've ever done, but once I started talking, everything gushed out. A tidal wave of relief washed over me as I told my true story at last. How every fibre in my body yearned for drink and the feelings of guilt and shame that followed. About the years I had felt this way but was too scared to admit my problem. And then I was no longer alone. I felt the warmth of Danny's hand holding mine tighter, as if giving me his approval to keep on opening the doors that had been locked for so long. I'm not a pretty crier, but Danny helped me wipe my tears as I apologised again and again, and each time he reassured me everything was going to be OK—I could beat this, he would support me every step of the way. Of course, it came as no surprise for Danny to hear I was out of control. He had seen me falling over, being sick and embarrassing myself enough times. But somehow he still wanted me. He still gripped my hand and talked about a time when all this would be behind us. What did I do to deserve this man, my loyal best friend? That night, when I shared my deepest, darkest secret and Danny didn't reject me, felt like a turning point in my life. He didn't cast me aside and go looking for someone better. I was important enough for him to stand by me. I had stopped believing in myself, but someone else still had faith in me.

After dinner I opened my laptop and searched for alcohol support in Stockton. I knew there would be plenty of demand for such a service. The actor Ross Kemp once came here to film a documentary about alcoholism. He was shocked to walk into a corner shop and find cans of cider on sale for less than a bottle of water.

'What chance do people around here have?' he said.

People in what seem to be hopeless situations drink to find some sort of release. It's the only thing they have. When you can't see a way out, you would rather not see anything at all. If you intoxicate yourself, the pain stops. Only it doesn't really. It comes back worse than ever, bringing all kinds of additional problems with it. The result was an all too familiar scene around Stockton, heavy daytime drinking, domestic violence, street brawls and petty crime.

The first service I found was CGL, the same support group as last time. I jotted down the number, feeling the drumbeat of my heart in my chest as I did so. And then I took a deep breath and dialled—only to be sent straight to voicemail. Great! I finally find the courage to seek help and there's nobody in! If I wanted a sign that I was meant to have a drink tonight, here it was. I mean, I did try. Then I remembered it was seven in the evening, well after office hours. Voice shaking, I left my name and number. And then I carried on as normal, drinking a bottle of wine and sneaking a second from under the sink. I often bought them and put them there so I could top myself up without Danny knowing. One bottle would look acceptable, but it was never enough for me.

The next day, I saw the charity's number flash up on my mobile and rushed down to the car park away from prying ears. They offered me a telephone appointment in three weeks' time. I wasn't expecting that—I thought they would strike faster. After all, three weeks was a lot of drinking time. Perhaps they were overrun with clients, or maybe they were giving me time to prepare and digest what was happening. Whatever the reason, to me, the delay meant just one thing—my final fling. Three weeks of solid drinking. Everything had come together—a green light from the professionals and annual leave from work.

Work that week was a blur as I functioned on autopilot to get me through the days. I went out almost every night and covered my desperation to drink with meals out and catching up with friends and family or whoever I could persuade to come out with me, before returning home for several nightcaps. After that I was on annual leave for two weeks, so we headed off down south in our camper van. Danny was always keen to go on a road trip, while in my mind it was just the chance for a final bender and to drink as much as I could. I bought crates of wine and cider and bottles of rum and whisky and spent two weeks hungover and anxious during the day and hammered every night. I pushed my addiction worries to the back of my head, refusing to acknowledge the enormous mountain I faced when I returned home.

I had booked my telephone appointment with the counsellor for 3pm one afternoon not long before the end of our holiday. From the outside, to our fellow campers, pausing to chat as they wandered around one of the most picturesque campsites we had ever stayed on, my life looked complete. It should have been. We were in beautiful, rolling countryside in the heart of Essex. Our camper van was on a perfect pitch at the water's edge and a glorious sun was beating down. Everyone was in holiday mode, walking around and checking each other's setups out. That's one thing I've always loved about camping. Strangers will make an effort to talk to you and share travel stories and tips. A few of us walked to the river's edge and I dipped my feet in the water while sipping a can of cider as I waited for the phone to ring. I watched the others with their drinks and wondered whether alcohol dominated their lives in the way it ruled mine. Then the call arrived and I slipped away to the privacy of a nearby bush. Can you believe that? I hid in a bush with my can of cider, making my introductions to an alcohol support worker. She asked how much I drank and how often, and about my mental health and what support I had. We chatted about my past and my drinking history, and she asked me to rate my feelings on a scale from one to ten. The tears flowed as I poured my heart out to this kind stranger, admitting out loud what I had kept secret in my heart for so long.

The conversation was unsettling and scary, but it also felt right. I had battled alone for too long. She made another appointment for me to visit the service and discuss my options in another two weeks' time. This sounded like another long gap with no further help, but I figured they must have known what they were doing. I pushed it all to the back of my mind and enjoyed the rest of my holiday, camping and getting drunk around open fires, two of my favourite pastimes. There was no need to worry anyway. I was simply learning some new techniques to manage my drinking. I would still have a drink at weekends, of course. For those two weeks, I continued to sicken myself with more alcohol. Deep down, though, I couldn't wait to get started. I felt ready.

Chapter Five

Confronting the Truth

We returned home from holiday and at nine o'clock on a sunny Monday morning, I went through my usual worries. Did I look like I'd been drinking all night? Was I sober enough to drive? And then I got into the car and headed to the clinic. I parked a few streets away and walked the rest. The fresh air would do me good, and I didn't want anybody to recognise the car or see me. It was my dirty little secret that I had let myself go and finally lost control of my life. I felt a disgrace, somehow weaker than 'normal' people. People who enjoy a few social drinks would say, 'Why don't you just stop? There's no need to get help. CGL? Isn't that where the druggies and drunks go?'

I walked up to the canary-yellow door and scanned both sides to see if anyone was watching as I rang the bell. A pigeon waddled over to join me on the doorstep. I wasn't sure if she was unwell or just there to give me moral support! Just as I stooped to stroke her, the door opened wide. I was taken into a small side room and told the nurse would come through to see me soon. I burst into tears as soon as I sat down. How the hell did I get here? How could I let this happen? I've let drink ruin my life. I'm the only person to blame. I chose this path of self-destruction. I should have noticed earlier. Drinking was supposed to be how I had fun. Instead, it had become a living nightmare. I knew I wasn't strong enough to get through this by myself. I felt miserable and inadequate. The runt of the litter, damaged and humiliated. I should have come here sooner. I had needed help for many years. I was addicted to alcohol. This was real. This was me. My life. I am an alcoholic. I couldn't bear to think of everyone talking about what had happened to me. 'Remember Lisa Peacock from school? Well, she's an alky now, you know.'

The receptionist interrupted my runaway thoughts by calling my name. Clare, the nurse I saw, was kind and reassuring. Everything is going to be all right, she said. She began by taking my blood pressure and then asked me to blow into a breathalyser. Shit! What if I am over the limit? Will she call the police? Will they arrest me for drink-driving? The fresh blouse I put on just half an hour ago was now damp with sweat. But to my amazement, the test was clear, and the horror of having to call my boss from the police station receded.

We talked about my drinking, and Clare asked what my goal was. She told me the best results were from people who abstained from alcohol for long periods. Is this woman suggesting

I stop drinking altogether? Nothing? Zero? For months? Is she mad? She talked of various options for quitting, such as residential and home detox, but her words washed over me. She might as well have been talking to the wall. I was still smarting about being told I wouldn't be able to simply reduce my drinking to normal levels. I felt overwhelmed and emotional. My heart thumped and I felt a wave of panic rising inside. *This isn't the right place for me. I don't need to stop—what's she talking about? I just want to be in control. I don't need bloody rehab!* I couldn't imagine a life without alcohol. No 'drinky-poos' with friends, no flute of fizz to celebrate the good times, no boozy days out, no Saturday liveners, no Sunday afternoon pints to finish my weekends off? What would be the point of living? Clare advised me to contact my GP for some thiamine tablets and start taking them as soon as possible. She told me they could prevent a type of brain damage caused by too much drinking. That sounded serious, and I made a mental note to buy some online later. Then she handed over some leaflets and asked me to visit my GP to have blood taken for tests, and she booked another appointment for the following week.

I walked back to the car, shoved the information into my glove box and went to work, making a lame excuse about having to go to the doctors. On the way home after my shift I bought two bottles of wine, then I nipped into the pub and drained a double whisky to smooth out the shockwaves flashing through my brain.

At home later that night, Danny and I looked at the leaflets they had given me. We looked at my options and the benefits and drawbacks of each one...

Residential detox

Pros: Away from home to think clearly. Dedicated time to concentrate. Twenty-four-hour support. There would be other people like me. They would medicate me to avoid the risk of seizures.

Cons: I would need a week off work. They had a long waiting list. Although I would have time alone to detox, it wasn't in my natural environment—would I need to learn all over again when I got back home to my usual surroundings?

Drink down: I would reduce my drink each evening, eventually down to zero. I would then be eligible for anti-craving medication, Acamprosate.

Pros: I wouldn't need time off work.

Cons: I'm an all-or-nothing person. I would rather have nothing than cut down. I have been trying to do that for years.

Drink down with medication at home: I would take a drug called disulfiram a few hours before I normally drank. If I drank even small amounts of alcohol, the medication would make me very ill.

Pros: It would deter me from drinking.

Cons: I know myself. I wouldn't take the medication.

Detox at home with medication: They would give me chlordiazepoxide to reduce the risk of seizure. After seven days, I would be eligible for anti-craving medication.

Pros: The medication would make me slightly drowsy.

Cons: I would need a week off work and a responsible adult with me constantly.

That's when it hit me like a sledgehammer. This was more serious than I thought. I had tried to moderate my drinking for years, but maybe stopping completely was the only way. My plans to continue drinking at weekends and other times were evaporating before my eyes. But medication? Was it really this bad? Could it be dangerous? Wasn't the whole approach a little drastic? The medication on offer all came with a risk of seizure and could make me violently sick. I might as well just keep bloody drinking, I thought. Danny didn't like the idea either, thinking we could manage my situation without drugs. I pretended to agree, knowing he didn't realise just how much I had lost myself, how every waking thought in my head led to booze. I was embarrassed we were even having this conversation. Having my guilty secret out in the open felt so raw. But Danny held my hand tenderly and assured me that everything was going to be all right. He would always be there to help and support me. I knew he would, but that wasn't what I wanted, Danny having to look after his poor useless girlfriend because she couldn't say no to a drink. I was a grown woman, for God's sake! And for all that Danny believed in me and was confident I could win this battle, I still didn't. Anyway, life could never be the same. That was one of the big differences between us. Danny exuded confidence and positivity, believing anything was possible. He had so much energy and an admirable can-do attitude. I wished I was more like him.

I still had a week to decide. I would try to limit my drinking and imagine my life without wine or cider or any alcohol at all. That might not sound so hard to some people, but booze had been my best pal for so long now, a close companion since I was a little girl. We had been through dark days together—break ups, anxiety, bereavement, mental health issues and every curveball life had thrown at me. We'd also been together for the good times, birthdays, weddings and any other excuse I could think of to celebrate. I had never lived without alcohol, so I didn't know any different. The thought of going through the rest of my life without it altogether filled me with fear and dread. My whole life was built on the unsteady foundation of booze.

After going over each option with a fine-tooth comb, I decided I would stop drinking for a year. It would be hard, but I told myself it was only twelve months out of an entire lifetime. I would retrain my brain. After a year, I would have cured myself and could drink in moderation, just like everyone else. Yes, the medication sounded drastic, but these people were professionals. They had been through this countless times before and knew what worked.

The next hurdle was telling my parents. But they enjoyed a drink most nights and just couldn't accept I was an alcoholic. For years, I had confided in them and told them I needed to reduce my drinking. But it seemed almost as though I was judging their drinking by giving up, like I was implying they should stop too. They had worked hard all of their lives, bringing us tearaways up, and now they were enjoying their retirement. I decided not to share too much with them. I had suffered mental health problems over the years, but Mam and Dad had never understood the torment in my head. They weren't to blame. Theirs was the you've-just-got-to-get-on-with-it generation. You didn't talk about your feelings. You swept them under the rug, dusted yourself off and moved on. That's not to say they weren't supportive. They had always been there for me, especially when I was a single mum, helping with babysitting while I worked to provide everything Jimi needed. In fact, I had taken advantage of their kindness over the years and put them through unimaginable stress during my teenage years. They were more like friends in many ways. All my friends wanted cool, easy-going parents like mine. As expected, they greeted my plan with a wall of negativity. Why are you doing that? What, stop altogether? You won't drink at all? What will happen after a year? It's almost Christmas, you can't start now! Would there ever be a good time? I didn't know any of the answers. I just knew I needed to stop. I couldn't go on feeling like this. I had to strike now. This was happening.

I would begin with a week-long home detox, with the help of sedative medication. After seven days, they would classify me as alcohol-free and I would qualify for anti-craving medication. I would always need a babysitter, so Danny would drop me at my parents' during the day and then pick me up after he finished work. I had no annual leave left, so I would have to lie and pull a sickie—I would think up an excuse later.

What would I tell Jimi? I had always been open and honest with him and didn't want to start keeping secrets now, but the truth is I was ashamed. The prospect of admitting that alcohol had taken such a grip on my life left me mortified. I was his mother and I should have been stronger. I should have been a better person. Tears streamed down my face whenever I even thought about what was happening to me. But I knew that honesty was the best policy. No more hiding. I needed to out myself. A family gathering at the table would be too dramatic. Determined to keep the conversation light, I arranged a trip to our local snooker centre. Just the two of us. I had been taking him there since he was six years old and he had become a useful player—I could never beat him. We enjoyed a couple of frames and I ordered a pint of cider to help with the nerves. Old habits, and all that. Then the time came to confess.

'Son, you know I like a few drinks and a laugh? Well, it's become a bit of a problem. I think I need some help. Professional help.'

I bit my lip and tried to hold back the tears as I waited for Jimi's response.

'For drinking?' he said, stunned. 'What, like rehab? I don't think it's that bad, Mam. You don't drink that much—you're not an alcoholic.'

This wasn't the time to hold back.

'Well, I think I do drink too much and it's getting on top of me,' I said. 'I feel like I can't stop any more. I've actually been in touch with someone who can help already. It's a place called CGL in Stockton. They help people with addictions.'

Then the questions started. Where is CGL? What do they do? Would I have to go away?

'No, I don't think so. I'm going to try to do it myself, at home. It's called detoxing. I have an appointment to find out more, but the plan is to stop drinking for a year. I need to give my body a break and teach myself I don't need to drink.'

I realised I hadn't looked him in the eyes once. Shame, deep, dark shame, was weighing me down.

'Good for you, Mam. I don't think you need help, but if you think you do then good on you for doing something about it.'

I'd raised him well. I grabbed him and kissed his cheek. This boy of mine has turned into a fine young man, so kind and caring. He hid his soft side behind his six-foot frame and handsome dark features, but he didn't fool me. I know it's there. When he was a little younger he saved all his pocket money to buy treats and toys for the local dog rescue centre. We found a box and wrapped it in colourful paper, trimmed it with tinsel and drove to the centre. His little face lit up when he dropped them off for the strays. I was so proud to call him my son. All I wanted was for him to be happy.

'I want you to be very careful,' I said. 'I don't want you to end up like me. Watch what you're drinking and look out for your friends, too.'

Jimi reassured me he was OK and promised to be careful. And that was it, short and to the point. I often found it difficult to talk to people about my thoughts and feelings. I become emotional and have to fight to hold back the tears. I suppose it's coming from a family of non-talkers.

'Your shot, Mam,' Jimi said. 'You're on yellow.'

I took my shot, my worries feeling lighter for having told him. Yes, my life was a shitshow, but I was doing something about it. This wasn't how I'd planned things. Telling someone who looked up to me that I had a drinking problem was one of the hardest things I'd ever done. I just hoped Jimi could learn from what was happening to me and avoid falling into the same dark hole.

I decided to take Danny with me to my next appointment. But when the morning came, I felt sick in the pit of my stomach. We sat in the car for a few moments after arriving. I felt beaten and broken. How could I do this to myself and to Danny and Jimi? Did they feel embarrassed about me? What if Jimi's friends made fun of him, all because of me? The tears streamed down my face. Danny walked round to the passenger door and opened it to let me out, otherwise I would still be there now. He took hold of my hand and I realised I was trembling so much, even my knees were knocking. If Danny wasn't there I would have tried to run away. Instead, I looked him in the eye and I grabbed his hand with both of mine, grateful for the support of this good, kind, strong man. I need his physical support as much as his emotional help. Without it I would have struggled to put one foot in front of the other.

As I knocked at the bright yellow door, I noticed an empty cider can discarded in a bush through the railings. Was this someone's last drink before detox? I burst out laughing, unsure if it was nerves or my twisted sense of humour. Just something silly that was enough to lighten my mood.

Inside, the same kind nurse sat down and started telling us what would happen next. She explained that the medication for my home detox is a controlled drug called chlordiazepoxide and would come in separate prescriptions lasting three days each. They would have to be collected from the chemist each morning. On day three, I would need to come back to the clinic for the next prescription. I was not to be left alone for seven days. My responsible adult would even need to check on me when I went to the toilet. He or she would need to know the signs of seizure and learn how to put me in the recovery position. Danny and I glanced at each other, but didn't say a word until we were outside. How on earth were we going to manage all that? Danny started work at seven, his job took him all over Scotland and the North-East of England. How could he wait until nine o'clock to collect a prescription and then get to the chemist? He wouldn't have time. I couldn't go, as I wasn't able to drive or be on my own. Danny had no annual leave left and we were already losing my wages. We couldn't afford to lose his income as well. I would have to ask my parents. They were both retired and would have time to help me. I knew it was a lot to ask, but it was only one week and they'd seen how much I struggled with booze. I still had to wait for two weeks before starting, but at least I had a date and was prepared. I knew I had a mountain to climb, but I was going to give it my best. I had to. This could be my last chance.

Chapter Six

Welcome to Booze Club

Sunday October 31st 2021 was the night before detox. I was at my parents' house, talking about what was about to happen. But Dad hadn't grasped how much I would need their help. They would have to leave me on Wednesday, he said, because they were dropping the car off for its MOT, and then they liked to go for a walk and look in the charity shops. I'd just told him I couldn't be left on my own!

'Mum, could you stay with me?'

She didn't reply. Perhaps I hadn't explained clearly enough. They certainly didn't seem to realise how serious this was. Dad wouldn't have his car, so I offered him mine to do the chemist runs.

'Why should I have to get up early?' he said.

I couldn't even summon up the energy to reply. My heart sank and I felt like my own parents had kicked me in the teeth.

I felt the heat rising through me and stormed out of the house before I said something I would regret.

'Why should I...?'—the words kept playing on a loop in my head. I had never felt good enough, always believing everyone else was better than me. I always had to try harder to be liked, trusted or respected. Now I had no value at all. I wasn't even worth the effort from my own mam and dad. This just confirmed what I had felt for years. I was an idiot, so stupid to think I could try to stop drinking. I had failed before I had even begun.

But slowly, as I paced the streets, my thoughts settled. With less than twenty-four hours to go before I started my detox, I needed to make another plan. I called my brother, Stephen, who often worked from home. He rearranged some meetings but couldn't commit for the full week. I even called Jimi, which was hard. I was supposed to be his caregiver, not the other way round, but I had been backed into a corner. Jimi was twenty by now. He would have helped, but he was working and had used up his annual leave. I thought about friends, but they all worked or had children. Come to think of it, I hadn't even told any of my friends. I drove home, hoping I was worrying about nothing. My parents would call, we would kiss and make up, and they would still help me. But the call never came and I cried myself to sleep.

***

Day 1

The moment I woke the next morning, I scrambled for my phone. Maybe I'd missed a call or a text message from Dad. But there was nothing. I dressed for work, my eyes swollen and red from crying and lack of sleep. Now I had a decision to make. I drove to the care home early and counted the minutes until nine o'clock when I could call Chloe, my support worker. All the old ladies wanted to know what was wrong—I looked like I'd done ten rounds in a boxing ring. I kept it simple and said I'd had a row with my family—if I had gone into any more detail I would have broken down. At a couple of minutes to nine, I made my way out to the car park, sat in my car and called Chloe. Knowing my family had let me down was bad enough, but saying it out loud and admitting it to someone else was even worse. I was a loser, with nobody in the world to help me. I wasn't worth the effort. I had also failed everyone who had helped me come this far. So many people had gone out of their way, doctors, nurses, key workers... Chloe couldn't believe what I was telling her. I could hear sympathy in her voice.

'You were so ready,' she said. 'What are you going to do now?'

In that split second, I made my mind up. I was going to continue with the detox plan, but I would do it myself. I wouldn't take any medication and would carry on working. I knew it would be the biggest challenge I had ever faced, but I would try anything. I felt backed into a corner and believed I had little choice. I wanted my life back. Chloe warned me about the risks of seizure, but they were risks I had to take. We planned telephone appointments for the rest of the week, and she wished me luck. I knew she meant it. At least someone was on my side. I sat in the car for a few more minutes before I dared return to work. I needed to take in my surroundings. I wanted to remember this moment forever. The day I changed my life. I was terrified about having a seizure, but I worked in a care home with 24-hour medical support. It was the safest place possible. I struggled to convince myself I was making the right decision. All I had to do was get through one week, seven days, 168 hours. How hard could it be?

For the rest of the day I busied myself with work, trying to focus on anything but the long, hard days that lay ahead of me. Colleagues had been giving me odd looks all day. They could tell I wasn't myself. I'm what people round here call a 'gobshite', loud and outgoing, so it was out of character for me to sit in my office working quietly. More often than not I was still slightly half-cut, larking around and being dramatic about how hungover I was. They were also used to me being an open book, sharing everything that happened in my life, but today I kept my lips sealed about what I was about to go through. Not only was I too embarrassed to tell anyone, it was also all too raw. As soon as I thought about the support I would need I welled up. I knew my whole life was at a crossroads.

At one o'clock that afternoon, I started thinking about having a drink. After all, now I was detoxing myself, could I just start next week instead? I didn't need any professional input.

My addiction was trying to talk me into drinking again. Then I remembered how I had been breaking the same promises to myself for twenty years. It was now or never. An email pinged in my inbox, reminding me of my first yoga class that night, which I'd forgotten. Apparently, I'd booked up for ten sessions. It's amazing the marvellous ideas you come up with when you're drunk! I searched for self-help books about giving up drinking, but they all looked too dry, if you'll pardon the pun. One stood apart from the crowd, however. The story was personal, a memoir instead of a textbook. I screenshot it for later. I was already worrying about not being able to sleep. I knew that was a classic excuse for drinking, the oldest one in the book. I planned to buy bagfuls of snacks and treats and stopped at a supermarket on my way home. I opted for a selection of tapas, sweet treats, face masks, moisturiser, a fluffy headband, a scented candle and some new pyjamas. Did you know a girl can conquer anything in new PJs? It's a thing!

The yoga session was in a spooky church and when I saw it I almost didn't go in. But although the building was dimly lit and uninviting, once inside, everyone was friendly and welcoming. And I was thankful for the moody, low-level lighting, as I had no idea what I was doing. If anyone had seen me I would have collapsed in a fit of the giggles! The instructor told us to focus on our breathing and I tried to relax, but kept finding myself looking around, slyly assessing which of the other ladies would have a few glasses of wine tonight. Probably all red wine drinkers round here in the posh end of town, I concluded. At the end of the hour, the instructor addressed the room.

'Come on ladies, grab your cuddle blankets,' she said.

You what? Nobody told me anything about bringing a blanket! It must be a joke! But then I looked around and saw a room full of grown adults curling up into the foetal position with snuggly fleeces wrapped around them. I tried not to laugh, but my jerking shoulders might just have given me away! Despite the session's weird ending, I felt better, and it had passed an hour without me having a drink.

Back at home, I took myself off for a bath. But what began as a relaxing soak ended in tears, my skin scrubbed until it was red raw and the water tepid around me. The craving was overpowering. My whole body screamed at me for a drink, just a small one, anything at all. The surface of my skin crawled and my heart pounded like a power drill burning out its motor. Beads of sweat dripped from my forehead as feelings of despair and hopelessness overwhelmed me. I wanted to turn off the lights and forget about the world. What had I done to myself? I summoned the strength to lift myself out of the bath and roughly towel-dried my hair. I put on my new pyjamas and felt a little fresher, although the sadness still hung around my shoulders like a shroud. I laid on my bed and downloaded an app called How Many Days? I'd used it before to count down to my holidays, but now it had another purpose. I had decided that for each night I didn't drink I would transfer £10 into a savings account. Who was this outrageous lie for? My bank manager or myself? The true figure I was saving was far more than that. Then I looked through my screenshots for the book I had seen, *The Sober Diaries*, by Claire Pooley. I left the book downloading and headed for a snack, but after devouring a tub of hummus and half a packet of crackers I was bored and looking around for something to do. I had never realised before just how much time I spent drinking. I made myself a cup of tea and drank it with a slice of cake. All I could think of doing was eating, especially anything sweet. I suppose it helped keep my hands busy. Eating this much was disastrous for my waistline, but I had bigger fish to fry right now and if I wanted a biscuit I would damn well have one. It was going to be a long night, and I was already worrying about how I would sleep. Why couldn't I just buy a bottle of wine? Lots of people drink every night. Was it really that bad if I just had one drink? My hands clenched into tight balls and a wave of anger surged through me. Everywhere I looked, Danny was there, checking I was all right. In the end, I snapped.

'Leave me alone!'

His only crime was trying to care for me, but at that moment in time he was the enemy, someone I could safely lash out at. He could have a drink and I couldn't. He wasn't addicted and I was, so I got out of his sight. I lay in bed drenched in my own sweat, my head full of writhing worms, punishing me with a mixture of negative emotions—anger, sadness, jealousy, hopelessness. I felt lost. I had failed. I wasn't good enough. I deserved to feel like this. I was to blame. I had done it to myself. I was the idiot. I needed a drink.

My heart raced so much that I didn't dare sleep in case the angry butterflies inside my chest gave up their fluttering. What if I had a heart attack and Danny just slept beside me, not realising I was dead? Should I wake him? Should I get up and drive to hospital? Or maybe I should just have a drink, and then it will all stop? I tossed and turned and then spent half the night in the bathroom curled up with a damp flannel on my forehead. Of course, I had stopped drinking for the odd night before, but it had never felt this bad. I felt winded, as if someone had sucked the life out of me. My drinking had worsened since the last time I'd stopped, which probably intensified the cravings. Perhaps it was also knowing I wouldn't be having a drink in a few days. In fact, I wouldn't be having a drink for 364 days. Deep into the early hours, I eventually cried myself to sleep.

***

Day 2

Danny was standing beside the bed with a cup of tea when I woke. I remembered. For the first time in days, I beamed, even with my thick head and lack of sleep.

'I did it!'

He kissed me on the forehead.

'You did, love, well done.'

I checked my app. One day. I don't know what else I expected it to say! It may not sound much, but it was to me. It was the start of something. Feeling excited now, I opened my banking app and moved my first £10 over to my savings fund. Then I dressed and headed off to work.

Chloe was calling me at lunchtime, so I got my head down and kept busy doing some filing until then. I usually put off the job and let papers pile high on my desk, but not today—my office had never been so tidy. One of my colleagues became suspicious and asked if I was leaving.

On the stroke of twelve I sneaked into the car park until Chloe's call. She asked how I was doing, and I told her about the previous night and my cravings. But she said I was doing well and reminded me I had a Zoom meeting that night. Damn! I had completely forgotten about that. I couldn't think of anything worse. I loved meeting people and wasn't afraid to talk about my problems, but I definitely preferred doing it in person rather than on a screen. But these online meetings were part of my 'contract' with CGL. I put it to the back of my mind and got back to work. I'd never enjoyed filing as much in my life, although I had a splitting headache. In fact, I felt like I was hungover.

When I got home I jumped into a hot bath, the bubbles reaching the brim. I had always been a bath person. It usually relaxed me. The bathroom in our cramped, one-bedroom flat was my only private space. But tonight it was just a corner of my prison. I lay there crying, fighting the familiar cravings and asking myself for the millionth time, how had I ended up here? If I had ever doubted I was addicted to alcohol, I no longer could now. I was a rattling wreck, a demon deep within screaming—'I need alcohol!' And then I remembered my Zoom call. I jumped out of the bath, grabbed a towel and scrambled for the laptop, logging in just in time and ensuring the camera was switched off as I dripped onto the floor. The meeting began and I braced myself to say those famous words, 'My name is Lisa and I'm an alcoholic.' But it didn't go like that. Instead, they asked us to think about how we might feel and how we could cope, and discussed techniques that could help in a crisis. They introduced us to the four-step TIPP system...

Temperature: A cooler temperature will slow your heart rate and can distract you from your thinking pattern. I could do this with a cold flannel, or just rinse my face under a tap.

Intense exercise: We can have built up energy from overwhelming emotions, and an intense burst of exercise can spend this energy. I lived in a block of flats, so I figured a quick burst up the stairs could help.

Paced breathing: Take a deep breath through your nose (abdominal breathing) for four seconds and then exhale through your mouth for six seconds. Do this for one-to-two minutes. This should help the physical side of your emotions. I could do this anytime—a tool to tuck away for my angry moments.

Progressive muscle relaxation: When we have extreme emotions we need to relax. You tense each part of our body from the head down, feel how tight you are and then loosen your muscles. This is another useful way to let go of any excessive energy.

I was glad I'd attended the meeting. I came to the realisation that I wasn't the only person in the world who was addicted to alcohol. I was just as guilty as anyone of subscribing to the popular stereotype of an alcoholic. I had never seen myself as an alcoholic, but that's what I was. It's such a dirty word, rarely spoken in polite society, but it shouldn't be. Most people are afraid to mention the subject, or they whisper the word under their breath. But alcoholics are normal people. We're not all lurking in the shadows or swigging cider from bottles in brown paper bags on park benches. We aren't losers, failures, under-achievers or down and outs. We are solicitors, carers, nurses, police officers, teachers, engineers and lollipop ladies. We are everyday people. We are everybody. We work hard and contribute to the community. We continue to function, nursing secret hangovers and wearing forced smiles to disguise our cravings.

I decided to call my weekly Zoom meeting 'Booze Club'. I know I probably shouldn't have, but you've got to laugh, haven't you? My family have always been good at making fun of ourselves. When you're faced with a shitty situation, we deal with it through jokes and craic. Well, this was a complete shitstorm, so Booze Club it was! I didn't say much in that first meeting. I just made notes in my jotter and doodled 'Booze Club' on the front cover. Why not? It's my jotter!

Afterwards, I put on my PJs and headed to the fridge, eyeing up a slice of black forest gateau. I needed sugar. Alcohol was going to be the least of my worries at this rate! I added a generous dollop of cream and it vanished in seconds. Wanting more, I went back and this time took the tray with the rest of the cake. I didn't even bother with a bowl, diving straight in with my spoon. The cravings were agonising. And then I felt the familiar wave of anger and resentment. Everyone else in the world could have a drink tonight. Why the hell couldn't I? My chest tightened and my lip curled. Heat seared through my veins. The walls of the flat felt as though they were closing in, like a scene in an Indiana Jones film. I needed some air. I quickly changed, snatched my car keys and handed my purse to Danny. I couldn't trust myself not to go to the shop and buy booze. I warned him not to give it back and said if I asked him to buy me booze, not to do it. He offered to come with me, but I needed some time alone. I drove to the beach in Redcar and parked up facing the sea. It was cold and dark. I shone my full beam on the ocean and watched its raging wild horses galloping towards me. I shuddered as I thought of all the lives the sea had taken through the ages. Then I switched off the lights and started crying. First came anger, then sadness and finally self-disgust. How pathetic I was, crying like a spoilt toddler because I couldn't have a drink. There were people out there with real problems. Serious illness, life-threatening diseases. I hated myself because I couldn't have a drink and I couldn't live without one. I took a deep breath, closed my eyes and focused. I am Lisa Peacock, I tell myself. I can do this. I am doing it. I summoned some strength from somewhere and headed home.

The drive back was slightly less traumatic. Danny was waiting and worrying. I wasn't sure if he was scared I had done something stupid or that I'd gone for a drink. I didn't ask. We sat down and I tried to explain what was happening to me. Opening up and saying how I felt about alcohol was all very new to me. Back in 2014, when I tried to give up for the first time, I kept my secret safely hidden from Danny and everyone else. And that was why it hadn't worked then. This time was going to be different. I was determined not to fail. Danny sat and listened, but I wasn't sure he was taking it in. How could he? How could he understand something as pathetic as me being sad because I couldn't drink? I wasn't just sad. I felt torn apart. My life lay shattered in pieces all around me. All hope was gone. Danny just reassured me everything would be OK and let me rant on. I told him I was constantly thinking about drinking. For years, I had tried to manipulate most situations towards drink. I turned quiet country walks into benders and quick Friday afternoon visits to the pub after work into all-weekend sessions. Something as healthy as kayaking ended up with a lock-in at the clubhouse or even the weekly grocery shop meant the reward of a pint or three afterwards. I would then get too drunk to cook and we would order a takeaway. Danny tried so hard to be supportive. He told me it wouldn't be like this forever. But to me, it was the end of the fucking world. I asked him to be patient with me. It wouldn't be easy. In the back of my mind, I wondered why he had stayed with me all these years. Why should he put up with all my problems? I loved him so much and I felt guilty for dragging him down with me. I thought about all the times I had let him down. The days out we had planned, only for me to be too hungover or too drunk or anxious to go. He deserved better than me. But I would be better.

My nerves frayed, I climbed into bed. But again, I barely slept. I spent the small hours staring at the ceiling. I thought about sneaking out to one of the two twenty-four-hour supermarkets near our flat. I could buy a bottle of whisky or rum and have maybe three capfuls, just enough to manage the pain, and then hide the bottle. I could stuff it in the cupboard behind the pile of Tupperware boxes and old takeaway containers we couldn't find lids for. It would be win-win—the pain would be over; my brain would temporarily cease its whirring and I could get a little sleep. Nobody would even know. Yes, it's drinking, but it's not a full bottle of wine. Anyway, maybe it wasn't a good idea to stop drinking alcohol altogether. Maybe I should cut down, little by little. Then I remembered Danny had my purse, and I'd made sure he kept it from me. I felt the breath wheeze out of my body, replaced with a red-hot burning rage in my chest. Tears started pouring as I made my way to the bathroom. I sat with my back to the cold, uncomfortable radiator and I clutched my knees to my chest. My body felt empty, just a shell. I had nothing left in me but pain and angst. I should end it all and let my family forget me. It will be tough for a while, but they'll get over it, eventually. And then I won't be a burden to them any more. I can't live with drink and I can't live without it—and I fucking despise myself for my weakness. I hate who I am. Then I thought of Jimi. I couldn't do that to him. I could never say goodbye. The door opened and Danny found me. Once again, he grasped my hands and helped me to my feet. Will this good man ever get sick of picking me up off the floor?

***

Day 3

I woke up and fist-pumped the air. I'd done it again. I transferred my £10 and checked the app. I knew it would say two days, but I needed to see it in black and white, my little reward. I felt proud but also nervous. I was only at the foothills of the steepest of mountains. Today was wobbly Wednesday, the middle of the week, and I was halfway there. Usually, it was the perfect excuse to have a drink. Eleven o'clock on a Wednesday morning in Stockton High Street was like a Saturday night. The tradition goes back to market days, but now it was just about getting pissed. Pubs advertised cheap drink offers and put on bandboxes to lure the punters in. By lunchtime everyone was drunk, their shitty lives put to one side for the day until the following morning, when reality would hit again. But I wouldn't be drinking with them tonight. As soon as thoughts of the weekend surfaced in my mind, I buried them again and threw myself into my work. I couldn't imagine how I was going to get through it. I wished I could sleep through until Monday.

I used to be first out of the door when my shift ended. Now I didn't want to leave. Work was my safe place, where my cravings were at their weakest. I couldn't talk about what I was going through there, as nobody knew. I wanted to keep it that way. I had enough going on in my head without having to explain it to my colleagues. I might tell them in time, I thought. I was amazed nobody had mentioned the difference in me. I was moody and snappy and didn't go into the staffroom for my lunch any more. I also sweated profusely.

As soon as I was home, I ran myself a bath. I put on my iPod and tried to relax. But it didn't work. I still felt a tightness in my chest that I feared could burst at any moment. And still I couldn't stop crying. This was rock bottom. I felt like I was nothing. I didn't ask for much in life. I just longed to feel fucking normal again. I wanted to leave this world of pain. I felt tempted to turn the hot tap on full, slip my head underneath the water, and disappear to somewhere peaceful where my torment would be over. I'd made a terrible mistake. I couldn't do this, not by myself, not without medication. I should have gone to a detox centre. I was in a terrible place. Everything was so pointless. Darkness, anger and sadness dominated my thoughts. I wanted to scream as loud as I could and smash the room up. I wanted to tear the sink out, rain terror on the toilet with a hammer and pull the radiator off the wall. My body trembled with fear as I gasped for breath. I sat up and tried to pull myself around, ripping out the plug and turning the shower on cold. The icy water took my breath away as it sprayed against my body.

Then I dried myself and I put on my pyjamas. I needed to get out again, anywhere away from the walls of the flat closing in on me. I told Danny what I was doing and grabbed the car keys. This time I headed for the Tees Barrage where I could walk on my own, allowing the freshness of the outdoor air to cool my swollen face. I had arrived and opened the car door by the time I realised I was still wearing my pyjamas. *Fuck, fuck, fuck!* I burst into tears. Not only could I not drink, I was also cracking up. Was this what a nervous breakdown felt like? What were my fellow Booze Club members feeling now? I didn't think any of them were wearing their nightwear and crying into a steering wheel. My life was pointless. Why was I even bothering? I might as well drive my car into the river. I would reverse back for a run up, slam my foot onto the accelerator, smash through the barrier and plunge my car deep into the icy water until I reached a place where the pain would stop. But I still had a fight left in me. There was still a tiny flicker of hope.

'Get up, Lisa!' I shouted out loud. 'Lift your head off this wheel! You are Lisa Peacock!'

I took a deep breath and called on every ounce of mental strength I could to lift my heavy head. Just then a shiny seal cub popped its head up out of the water and stared right at me with its big black eyes. I smiled. I wondered if he heard me crying and came up to see me. Was he here to save me? I took his appearance as some sort of sign. He helped me to take a few more deep breaths. Again I repeated to myself, *I am Lisa Peacock. I can do this.* I am doing this. It was something I'd done in the past when

I needed to summon some inner strength. My mantra. Saying my name out loud somehow helped me. I can't explain why, it just does. It made me feel a little braver, pumping some energy back into my depleted batteries. So I would keep saying it. I just wouldn't tell anyone.

Back home, I got ready for the long, sleepless night ahead of me. I wondered which shops were still open selling booze. Not sleeping had always been an excuse to drink. Danny comforted me as I lay in bed, crying.

'I'm struggling, love,' is all I could say.

Danny climbed in behind and hugged me close.

'It's OK,' he said.

But was it?

***

Day 4

Thursday arrived. I liked daytime. Nights seemed to swallow me up, an endless, joyless, ghost train through the darkness. But the days didn't hurt as much. I checked the app and transferred my £10. I had £30 saved now. I could have bought three bottles of my favourite rosé wine with that. I suppressed that thought and got on with my daily routine.

At work, somebody asked if I was leaving again.

'No,' I said. 'Why do you ask?'

'Because your office has never looked so clean and well organised!'

I thought I'd always been organised. In reality, I'd just been managing. Barely scraping the surface of my work. Putting jobs off because I couldn't concentrate. Unmotivated and nursing daily hangovers. In fact, I still struggled to concentrate. Although I hadn't had a drink, I felt groggy and confused, with regular headaches. I had expected an instant dividend with a renewed vigour and clarity of thought. But not sleeping was taking its toll. After the turmoil of the night before, I changed tactics. I texted Danny and told him we were going out. I didn't care where, I just needed to stay out of the flat. Those walls wouldn't come in for me tonight. I stayed at work for an extra hour, just to avoid going home. Then Danny picked me up and we headed out.

'Where are we going?' I asked?

'To the beach,' he said.

I didn't tell him I had gone there on Tuesday night. He chose a different part of the coast, Saltburn, with a beautiful pier that offered stunning views of the moonlight shimmering on the water. Danny parked facing the sea. Despite the early evening hour, darkness enveloped the car and the cold was piercing.

'We should have brought a flask of tea,' I said, showing my age. We dared each other to run to the chip shop, and I somehow drew the short straw. Wasn't he supposed to be running around after me? I'm the one detoxing! I zipped my coat to the top and fastened the hood around my face. Then I sprinted to the kiosk, returning a few minutes later with two steaming white bundles. The mouthwatering aroma of fish, chips and vinegar filled the car. Afterwards, Danny switched on the engine and shone the car lights onto the waves crashing in towards the beach. One was so big it splashed the bonnet of the car, causing me to scream with shock before we both burst out laughing. This was just what I needed. To experience laughter again. To feel normal. To step out from the cramped detox box in my head. I stopped laughing and took a moment to look into my man's handsome face, his big brown eyes locked onto my stare. He still looked at me in wonder, as he always had, and I could see his eyes were ablaze with love. Danny didn't say too much. He wasn't what you called a talker, he was a doer. But at this moment, we didn't need any words. I felt so proud to call this good man my partner. This was the person I wanted to spend the rest of my life with. I wanted to see every inch of the world with him, and to watch each other's hair turn grey (or in my case, greyer). He made me aspire to be a better person. He gave me courage and hope. He wasn't going anywhere. He was here with me now, in the brokenness of the weakest moments of my life. He saw I was vulnerable and he had me. Whatever happened from this moment on, I knew he would be there. If I fell, he would catch me. When I cried, he would wipe away the tears. He would help me put the pieces back together and be the person I longed to be. My heart burst with love for him. As we headed home and my thoughts turned to my next restless night, I thought of the others at Booze Club and wondered if they were doing this alone. I was so glad I had Danny here. I didn't think I could have managed it by myself. Without him in my life, I would have sunk beneath the waves years ago.

Chapter Seven

Fizzy Pop in a Fancy Bottle

I had been dreading Friday. When it finally arrived, I wished I could take a magic pill that would transport me to Monday morning. Who even says that? At one time, the Boomtown Rats' I Don't Like Mondays could have been my theme tune, and now I couldn't wait for the weekend to be over. I felt groggy and lacked the usual skip in my Friday step. I checked my counter app. Four days. I couldn't remember the last time I'd gone this long without a drink and I managed a weak smile as I moved my £10 over. I felt exhausted from lack of sleep, but I reasoned I could sleep when I was dead. The constant crying had also left me dehydrated. I wondered if wine has any hydration properties. It must have something. I also stank. All I did was sweat and my clothes clung to my body. My skin looked terrible, red, blotchy and clammy, and no amount of makeup seemed to make me look human. Constantly jumpy and on edge, I tiptoed around the flat as though scared someone was going to leap out of the wardrobe at me. Paranoid in my own home. When, if ever, would I feel normal again?

Even my office wasn't the haven it had been. My safe space had been shattered, and everyone was getting on my nerves. Everything was going wrong. I hurled my stapler across the room, leaving a tiny dent in the wall. All I could hear was people making weekend plans. I don't want to know about your shopping trip to Leeds and all the cocktails you're going to drink! I loved Leeds and I loved cocktails. Some of the other girls were planning a few drinks after work. I prayed they didn't ask me, not knowing what I would say. I would either burst out crying or sprint for the pub ahead of them! Thankfully, my moody ways had consigned my invitation to the bin. How am I going to cope? How will I live with nothing? Weekends were for drinking. A day at the footy with a few pints, shopping and cocktails with the girls, watching Jimi play football with a couple of liveners in the club house, a hot tub with champagne, a barbecue with a crate of beers, a picnic with a few vinos, Pimm's on the lawn... you name it, and I would provide the drinks! I felt the now familiar tightness in my chest. I considered buying cocaine, just a couple of lines to take the edge off. Then I could still go to the pub, I'd just have soft drinks. It was terrible idea and I knew it. What was the point of stopping one bad habit only to start a worse one? If only I had that anti-craving medication, I'd be able to cope better. I turned off my PC and headed home. Jimi called to see how I was getting on. He was such a sweet, caring kid. I say kid; he towered over me. I felt a pang of guilt, hearing him having to check up on his mum.

'I'm doing OK,' I told him, managing to sound cheerful. 'And when I feel better, we can get together.'

What I didn't mention was I wanted to die. I was worried sick he would end up like me. I hoped I hadn't handed him the alcoholic baton. I regretted all the times he had seen me drunk. Don't get me wrong, he had never seen me at my worst, completely bongoed and unable to function, but he had often seen Mummy slurring her speech after one glass of wine too many. I resolved to have a heart-to-heart with him, but this wasn't the time. My nerves were shredded.

I came up with a plan to keep so busy that night I wouldn't even have time to think about drinking. I would clean the flat from top to bottom and then declutter. Tidy life, tidy mind. I started with the kitchen and began emptying all the cupboards. Danny returned home to a front room filled with tinned food, cleaning products, tea towels and all kinds of assorted bits and pieces. Luckily, we only had one drawer. My parents had six drawers in their kitchen, one for cutlery and five for junk. Dad still had mobile phones from the nineties! Thinking of Mam and Dad made me feel sad. I missed them. But I didn't have time for emotions that night. I had a spice rack to sort out. I threw out a few that had dried up and some were duplicates, so I tipped them into the other jar to make one. I found sassafras and galangal. I had no idea what either of them were, what you could make with them or how they'd found their way into my cupboard. I certainly couldn't recall buying them. I would look them up on Google later.

The tin cupboard was next. I slung the out-of-date rice pudding and rusty-bottomed tins of tomatoes in the bin and put the remaining tins back in the clean cupboard, with all the labels facing outwards. I chuckled to myself as I remembered the scene in the film Sleeping with the Enemy where Julia Roberts does the same thing. Under the sink next. I found three tins of furniture polish, five tubes of superglue and enough dishcloths to carpet the flat. I also found twelve sponges. I'd always felt anxious whenever I got down to the last one. Apparently, Mam suffered from the same anxiety. I had so much surplus cleaning stock that I made my brother a hamper. Imagine his joy! I emptied and cleaned the fridge, and I scrubbed the oven until it gleamed. It had never looked so good.

Later, I stuffed myself with anything sweet—chocolates, cakes and waffles—until I made myself feel sick. I would have tried anything to take the cravings away. They were taking over my mind and body until I couldn't concentrate on anything else. It absorbed every thought until I had nowhere else to go. This was real pain, physical and mental, and I couldn't turn it off. When I'd stopped smoking ten years ago I craved cigarettes all the time, but by this time I wouldn't thank you for one. I could only dream that one day it would be the same for alcohol. Exhausted, I curled up in bed and cried myself to sleep again.

I felt good on Saturday morning. I checked my counter app. Five days. I enjoyed an unexpected wave of satisfaction and moved my £10 over. Fifty pounds saved and a drink-free Friday under my belt. That was a major milestone. But there was also sadness as I realised this was probably the first Friday I hadn't drunk in eighteen years. I pushed the feeling aside. I had plenty to keep me busy that day, starting with the weekly shop. Was I over the limit to drive? Nope! Did I have a raging hangover? Nope! Still bright and early, I was in the supermarket, hair and makeup done. I sauntered around the shop like a proud peacock (pun intended!). I usually raced around in a huff, my hair scraped back and no makeup. But not this week. I found myself looking around hoping to find someone I knew, just so I could say, 'Me? No, I didn't bother having a drink last night. You?' But I didn't bump into anyone and without noticing, I was in the aisle. You know. The one we spent a quarter of our shopping budget on. Subconsciously, I had gravitated towards the drinks section. The bottles were so attractive, with fancy glass and trendy labels. All the fancy rosé wines standing to attention, shoulder to shoulder. 'Pick me, pick me!' they shouted. 'I'll be your best friend tonight.' I closed my eyes and imagined the pink liquid running down my throat. That first icy glass from the fridge after a long day. That hit off the first few mouthfuls. I licked my lips. It would have been bliss. I chastised myself and continued to the spirits aisle. The tequila, with his fancy sombrero. Jack Daniels promising a wild night. I walked on and ended up in the soft drinks section. Having always shunned this before, I am surprised at what delights I find—alcohol-free cider, wine, lager and even zero per cent gin! I mean, who knew?

I'm shocked. I didn't know these things existed. I'm even more taken aback when I see the prices. The same as normal booze, but there's no alcohol inside them! I opted for a zero per cent chardonnay and made my way to the checkout. The lady asked me for ID. Well, for one I'm forty-three, and secondly I don't have any fucking booze! Apparently, you need to look over twenty-five to buy alcohol-free wine as well. I didn't need any ID, though. I removed my face mask and she soon realised I was definitely old enough to drink fake booze.

Back home, I unpacked the shopping and saw Danny examining the pretend wine, pondering his next words. Was he wondering if I have given in? He opted for a safe, 'What's that?' and I told him.

'Apparently, it tastes and looks like wine, but there's no alcohol.'

'But should you be drinking that? Isn't it like tricking yourself into thinking you're having a drink? Maybe you should ask your support worker.'

I hadn't thought of it like that, but I couldn't call Chloe on a Saturday. I searched the internet but abruptly stopped myself. When I quit smoking, I had a little white inhaler. It didn't contain anything but helped with the hand-to-mouth habit. What harm could it do? It was fizzy pop in a fancy bottle, for goodness sake! I was having it. Feeling naughty, I poured some into a wine glass and sipped. Hmmm. It wasn't quite like the wine I was used to. Didn't seem to have the same kick.

We enjoyed a nice meal and settled down to watch a film. I can't even remember what it was, I was so distracted with my cravings. Whenever they got too much, I made my excuses and headed for the loo to hide out. Danny wasn't drinking in the flat. He wanted to support me as much as he could. I felt tremendous guilt but was also very relieved. If I'd had to watch him drink, well, I'm not sure what I would have done. It wouldn't have been pretty.

My bathroom had become an emotional battleground for me, my only hideout. I curled up on the floor, hoping the mat was clean but not caring too much if it wasn't. The cravings were too strong. I felt lice crawling under my skin all over my body. My head was so itchy I wanted to pull my own hair out. My chest was tight with fury. I cursed everyone in the world who was enjoying a drink at that moment. I thought of words, nasty swear words. I grabbed my phone and typed them in. Some formed a sentence, some didn't. It didn't matter much. What was important was getting them out of my head. It helped a little and I managed to sit up on the loo, where I came up with this...

You're getting on my nerves, I'm going for a walk,
I'm trying to cope with cravings, and all you do is talk.
I could pull my own hair out and kick and shout and scream,
I haven't slept for days and I'm splitting at the seams.
All I want is a vino, a whisky or pint,
I feel almighty rage, and my chest is getting tight.

I'm sitting on the toilet with my head in my hands,
Nobody can see it but the alcohol demands.

Saturdays were my wildest nights and my itch to party was always scratched. Now I needed to learn to live differently. All I wanted to do was sleep. Sleep was my only respite, the only peace I got, the land where I could forget the pain and angst. But it was hard to come by. Every night was torment, leaving me desperate for rest. I wondered if the doctor would prescribe me sleeping tablets. I mean, I could have even picked up the phone to a dealer and got some delivered, but I knew that wasn't the answer. I had to learn to live without emotional crutches. I was going to take this year out—no parties, no drink and no drugs. What would life be like without them? So far, it had been sheer hell. But it had to get better. Right?

Sunday morning came. I checked the app. Six days and £60 saved. We were going on a hike. I had always loved walking, ever since discovering the joy of the outdoors in the army cadets when I was a kid. We went on long treks, orienteering, kayaking, climbing, survival camps and shooting. I loved it and I was a natural—I could even hold my own on the shooting range. But over the years, my go-for-it adventurous nature had changed. I shied away from walks and days out because I was too drunk, hungover or anxious. Weekends had been dedicated to recovering from hangovers and planning my next drinking session. But not today.

We headed out to Roseberry Topping, the famous North Yorkshire landmark that I always thought resembled a frozen wave. I had scrambled up there many times, but not for about five years. We had picked up the family dog, who was a good distraction for me. His name was Jesus. I know. But we hadn't named him. We found him in the remote Bulgarian village of Velchevo while we were travelling in 2019. We had taken an old Land Rover Defender on a road trip, driving through seventeen countries and camping wild as we soaked up different cultures.

We were out walking and the dog's skinny frame just kept popping out of random bushes and he would run up to us, bobbing from side to side. Turned out he was a stray, living in abandoned houses and rummaging through bins for food. Even though his life had been tough, he always wagged his tail. In fact, he wagged it so much his whole body moved with it. The locals told us they found him with his three sisters in a plastic carrier bag inside a bin. He was the only one who survived. The villagers named him Jesus because of the white cross-shaped marking across his chest. We fell in love with him. We knew we couldn't take him on the rest of our journey, as he wouldn't fit in our truck, so we decided to send him back to the UK to live with my family. Our budget was already overstretched, so we organised a Go Fund me appeal. We needed £400 for transport, a doggie passport and vet's bills. We named the page 'Save Jesus', which certainly got people's attention. The appeal raised £150 and I stumped up the rest. Thanks to the power of Facebook, I found an expat who regularly drove to the UK to collect furniture for expats moving out there. His van was empty on the way over, so he delivered stray dogs. I packed

Jesus up with food, water and his new documents and he arrived in the UK just before midnight, just minutes before the UK's borders were locked because of the pandemic. Jesus was now loved by all. He even had a part-time job going into the care home. He was the perfect therapy dog because he was so chilled and loved cuddles and attention.

We parked up and started the 320-metre climb up Roseberry Topping. Within a few minutes I was out of breath, even though we were still on flat ground. A couple of ladies in their mid-sixties overtook us. They were chatting away, and my chest was on fire. They smiled sympathetically, no doubt thinking how pathetic I was for letting myself go. Fuck you! I'll show you! I thought, and then immediately felt guilty. The truth was, they probably didn't think that at all. It was all in my own head.

After a series of 'I can't breathe!' stops, we finally made it to the top. My lungs burned and I sat down to catch my breath. It had taken me seventy-five minutes, but I was there, and I stood up to mutter a triumphant, 'Stick that in your pipe and smoke it, you old grannies!' But my legs were shaking like jelly and I quickly sat down again.

The view from up there was spectacular. I could see the whole of Teesside and out to the coast on one side and miles of rolling Yorkshire hills on the other. I made a promise to myself that day. It was a promise I had made and broken many times. I was going to get back into shape. I was going to be fitter, stronger and better—and I was going to get up this hill faster next time!

For the rest of the day, we worked on our Land Rover. It kept me occupied, but I was also reminded how I used to do this with a bottle of cider in my hand. We would work on the truck and then finish our afternoon off in the pub, plotting our next camping trip on the back of a beer mat, or dreaming of packing it all in and going off travelling together again. I had made some great decisions in pubs—house moves, car purchases, travel destinations and career changes. I wondered if things would ever be the same again. Alcohol was ingrained on my brain, part of my DNA. How could I undo a lifetime's work? That night I slept well for the first time in a week, exhausted from my mountaineering. Giving up booze was pushing a heavy boulder up the biggest mountain I had ever faced. I just hoped the view at the top would be worth it. I was already battered, bruised and exhausted. And I was still on the flat ground.

Chapter Eight

The Keys to the Chocolate Factory

On Monday morning I checked my counter app. Seven days. I will say that again for dramatic effect—seven whole days! That's a week, don't you know? I half expected a trumpeter to burst into the bedroom and deliver a fanfare to celebrate my success. But only a week had passed. I had fifty-one more to go. I had fantasised about getting to the end of the year. I was in Florence, sitting in a trendy bar and ordering a crisp white wine with a side of cannoli. It would still be warm and I could sip my wine with my sunglasses on, looking all slim, suave and sophisticated. I would only have one glass, though. I would have learnt my lesson by then.

Today also marked me being officially alcohol-free. I now qualified for anti-craving medication, which I had been waiting for all week. Something to soften the ride. My body's craving for alcohol was all-consuming. It wasn't as simple as just not drinking; my body needed the drug. The temptation to reach out and grab that very thing I knew would soothe me screeched through my whole body and dominated every waking thought. My heart had been racing at a frightening rate all week. There's a reason people called it 'the cure'. Having a few drinks would have made all the withdrawal symptoms stop. Without it, I felt nauseous every day, exhausted, head aching, sweating, dehydrated and unable to concentrate. The mental aspect was the hardest for me. I can only describe what was going on in my head as hell. There was no getting away from it, no hiding place. I have heard it being described as 'the horrors'. It felt as if I was slowly moving through a never-ending nightmare, without any glimpse of hope.

    I crept towards the yellow door and checked behind as usual to see if anyone was watching me. Once inside, Clare took my blood pressure. It was a little high. Of course it was! It had been racing through my veins! She reached for the breathalyser and this time I wasn't nervous. No alcohol there. No, siree! I left with the green prescription slip, gripping it like Charlie Bucket with his golden ticket. As I far as I was concerned, I might as well have had the keys to the chocolate factory. I noticed my whitened knuckles on the steering wheel as I sat in the car park, steeling myself to go into the chemist. The second I handed that ticket over, somebody else would know. The staff were trained and would know what the medication was for. I shook my head. Why did I feel like this? If I had quit smoking I wouldn't have felt embarrassed buying nicotine patches, so why did I feel such shame now? I knew I had a problem and I was dealing with it. It takes guts to admit you needed help. And yet alcoholism was still taboo. I felt frowned upon. You get a pat on the back when you quit smoking, sharing your progress on social media. Why was this so different? Or was this just me feeling paranoid, terrified by my shame?

I edged towards the counter and recognised the lady serving. She saw me. Great! I couldn't turn around now. I cursed myself for going local. I should have driven out of town. Well, here goes, I'd better suck it up...

'Hiiee!'

My voice came out all high pitched. Anyone who knows me will laugh at this thought. After years of smoking and boozing, I usually sounded more like Barry White. We exchanged fake pleasantries and I handed over my prized golden ticket. She looked down, read it and then gave me a sly glance. I knew, she knew, and she knew I knew she knew. Like a bad Two Ronnies' sketch.

'It'll be ready in twenty minutes.'

I slunk off to the clothing department. I seemed to have swapped buying vino for picking up fluffy nightwear and cake. After collecting my medication I didn't waste time, popping two into my mouth in the car park and leaving these babies to do their magic while I got to work. I consciously avoided reading the warning label. Reading it would guarantee I would endure every side effect they on offer.

Tonight was yoga night. I nicknamed one girl in the class Moonhead (to myself, obviously). She was around twenty-ish but she was immature and talked far too much, yapping on during moves. I felt the urge to shout shut up. She was messing with my chakras, whatever that meant. What made it worse was she was ace at Yoga, her size-eight frame flawlessly performing every move, while I tried to manoeuvre my belly out of the way to get into position. I was trying to relax and be all Zen, but she was getting on my nerves. I mean, I could be loud, but I knew when to turn it off. Or did I? I wondered how many people I had upset over the years, especially when I was tipsy. I winced and tried to blank the thought out. I closed my eyes as we thanked Mother Earth for our being. This was going to be a marathon journey.

Later, I sat with my camera off again during Booze Club—seeing myself on screen would just make me self-conscious and distract me. Holding the laptop on my knees while sitting up in bed was awkward, especially since my little flat wasn't designed for Zoom calls. During the hour that followed, the facilitator asked us to write a list of things that were important to us. I made mine, in no particular order:

Family
Partner
Friends
Fitness
Travel

Music
Being charitable
Being honest and kind

The group leader asked us each to talk about what we had written and why they meant so much. Once we had all had our turn explaining, she asked us if we thought we had missed anything off our list. Nobody answered. She then told us something was missing and asked if anyone could think what. I quickly twigged what was missing from mine and raised my hand like a kid in the back of a classroom. 'Pick me, miss!' But I wasn't a kid, and I wasn't at school.

'I know what's missing,' I said aloud.

'What is it, Lisa?' she asked.

'It's wine. There's no alcohol on my list.'

'Exactly,' she replied.

It had caught everyone out. I thought drinking was my first love, but it turns out it wasn't even in the same division as the important things in my life. Was it so much second nature that I didn't even think about it any more? It had just become a part of me. But I still took this as a little boost. I was all about the small wins, anything to give me a lift and get me through the day.

The days passed by more quickly now, and I noticed a big change in my emotions. My anger seemed to have calmed a little, but sadness had replaced it. I couldn't quite put my finger on why my mood was so slow, but I felt like I had lost something and I moped around like a lost soul. Of course, I had lost something. Party Lisa was dead, and I was in mourning. What had once been a life built around alcohol was now a desperate attempt to live without it. A gaping hole tore through my world. I was trying to say goodbye to the old me and bury my addiction. No. I wanted it cremated, so it couldn't rise up and bite me on the arse again. I sulked, convinced my life had come to an end, but constantly reminded myself it was only for a year. A twelve-month lesson in self-control.

Chapter Nine

Shake a Tail Feather

Eleven days sober and I had a midweek date planned with a girlfriend. We were going to see a Tina Turner tribute act. The venue was the Globe Theatre in Stockton, newly reopened after many years and millions of pounds spent on renovations. I was eager to have a look around. The theatre had hosted famous names including The Rolling Stones, Buddy Holly, The Beatles and The Animals. I felt a pang of nerves and dread as I got ready for my first dry night out. It was midweek, so not as much pressure—good practice for a proper night out. I drove for once, and after we arrived, I sent my friend to the bar, but she raised her eyebrows when I asked for a Diet Coke. I hadn't confided in any of my mates. I wouldn't say I was being secretive, but I had certainly played the situation down. I had enough to focus on without having to explain myself to anyone. Anyway, it was hard enough for me to understand what was going on. Experience had also taught me a valuable lesson. Not to divulge everything about myself. Some people had thrown my vulnerability back in my face in the past. A friend once explained it to me as having a large, beautiful garden. Of course, people could visit my garden and share its space sometimes, but they didn't need to see all of it. That roped-off private section only belonged to me. My VIP zone. Invitation only. I gave her the universal sign for 'I'm driving,' mouthing the words as I did so. I looked around and admired the art déco building's intricately detailed coving. It was beautiful, but not what I had been expecting. With its shades of green and marble floors, it reminded me of the Emerald City from the Wizard of Oz. I had imagined more red, velvet and gold. Photographs of famous acts that had played there lined the walls, and I noticed two older ladies giggling like little girls. I couldn't resist walking over to them and I asked if they had been here in its 1960s' heyday. They enjoyed telling me how they both worked in the now long-gone Sparks Bakery and would save their wages to buy new dresses and the latest records. They would take the bus to the Globe every weekend and waited at the stage door to meet the Beatles on November 22nd, 1963, the day President Kennedy was assassinated. I loved listening to them reminisce. They told me the building looked almost identical, with just the odd new fixture. I wished them an enjoyable evening and searched for my friend. The bar was three-deep, but eventually we sat down and the show started. The first half dragged on. I wasn't fully engaged in what was happening on stage. I was too busy looking around the venue, assessing how many ladies were drinking wine or gin. The interval was nothing like what I was used to. It seemed to last forever, and I was twitchy and nervous. Usually, I sprinted to the loo and then to the pre-booked interval drinks area, searching the trays of delights for my name and then claiming my two large glasses of wine. But not tonight. The show restarted and the music picked up pace as Fake Tina pulled out the big party pieces. Sober Lisa sat tapping her foot, but party Lisa wanted to down a pint of wine and high-kick across the stage, showing the audience how to shake a tail feather. Sober Lisa won out. The night ended, and I had a stupid grin on my face. I was out, and I wasn't drunk—not even a sip. I barely slept that night, but this time it wasn't because I craved a drink. I was on a high because I didn't have one. Lisa 1, Vino nil points.

That weekend was Remembrance Sunday. I had tried to mark the occasion every year since I had illegally joined the Army Cadets when I was eleven. You were supposed to be thirteen, but I lied. I wanted in. I lasted three weeks until they found out, and then I had to wait two whole years to rejoin. I wasn't much of a soldier. Well, that's not quite true. I was fine with the action side—making fires, shooting and swinging from trees—but I hated being told what to do. I had no rules at home, so why would I listen to strangers? I was forever doing fatigues—boring jobs sometimes given out as minor punishments—and I got so used to painting fences I became a decent painter. We seemed to be constantly doing marching practice in the run-up to the Remembrance Sunday Parade. It might surprise you how many people struggle to march. They lift the same arm as the same leg, which is called tick-tocking. Try it!

The sound of the bugle playing the *Last Post* always brought back fond but also sad memories. I couldn't help but shed a tear when the crowd stood still and silent for two minutes. I have never lost anyone in war, but I could always feel the pain in the people around me and sense their loss. I usually went to the pub after the ceremony and sat with some of the older generation, buying them a pint or breakfast and listening to their war stories. I once ran into a guy who helped sink the *Bismarck*, on May 27th 1941. I will never forget the date, as it's my birthday—May 27th that is, not 1941. He was aboard *HMS Dorsetshire*, the heavy cruiser that finished off the "unsinkable" German battleship only ten days into its maiden voyage. He was an absolute joy to be with, wonderful company and full of amazing stories. The veterans packed out The Last Post, a local bar that gave them free port. Some of them drank to remember, while others drank to forget. Danny was in the forces and I sometimes thought this was the only day in the year he let himself remember some of the horrors he experienced. He joined the army in 2002 at the tender age of seventeen and served for six years, which included two tours of Iraq. I knew he missed the camaraderie of army life and Remembrance Sunday was when he got to meet up with like-minded people, raising a toast to friends they had lost. Although a sad time, there's always lots of banter as well. But I just couldn't face it this year. I felt guilty, but I was already too emotional and the thought of seeing so much sadness, not to mention watching everyone else booze all day, was just too much. Instead, I stocked up on sugary treats and watched the Queen lay her wreath at the Cenotaph from the comfort of my sofa.

Chapter Ten

Cold Turkey

I would like to say the first few sober weeks of my adult life passed by in a flash, but they didn't. They were long, drawn-out, painful days and gruelling, tear-filled nights. Every time I thought I had overcome the challenge I remembered I had to keep going. This wasn't a quick fix, like a fad diet. This was my life. I wanted to tell Mam and Dad I hadn't had a drink for several weeks. I had grown closer to my parents over the years. I needed them more than my three brothers did. Mam and Dad did so much for me when Jimi was born, decorating our home, supporting me financially and helping with childcare. I had watched Dad go through a triple heart bypass and seen Mam beat breast cancer. I struggled to cope with seeing them unwell. I once bought Mam a tiny book of sentences saying in so many ways how much I loved her and was grateful she was my mother and my friend. I tried to read a couple of lines out, but we both walked away, crying and laughing at each other. I tried again, only to burst out crying and laughing again. In the end I threw the book at her and said she would have to read it herself! I missed them.

I muddled through another week and somehow made it to Saturday. I had a night out planned with some girlfriends. A turkey-and-tinsel-themed birthday celebration in a boutique hotel. I was dreading going, not because I didn't want to see my friends, but because I didn't want to see them drinking. To make matters worse, I also looked and felt terrible. Outside, a storm was raging, and the newsreaders urged us to 'stay safe'. I hated that phrase, but it gave me the perfect excuse not to go. But after some thought, I decided I just couldn't let my friends down. Anyway, I couldn't shy away from weekend nights out forever. I needed to put a brave face on and deal with it.

We hadn't seen each other for some time. I got ready, carefully applying makeup to cover the dark circles under my eyes. My lack of sleep was showing. Walking to the car, the wind wasted no time messing up my meticulously curled hair. I arrived and everyone looked fantastic, all sequinned-up for the festive season. There were ten of us. I took my seat at the end of the table, feeling like an outcast. I ordered a Diet Coke, and of course, the girls ordered prosecco. It was a nauseating kick in the guts and I was green with envy. I couldn't tear my eyes away from them, pouring the liquid into their fancy crystal flutes and I watched enviously while they sipped, all feminine and fun. I could almost taste the cool bubbles on my tongue. I wasn't so sure those tablets were working. I didn't even want a full glass, just a tiny sip. It would be a long night. One girl spotted my soft drink.

'You not drinking, Lise?' she asked, using the shortened name for every Lisa in the world.

'No,' I said. 'Driving.'

'Well, why don't you just have one? One is OK!'

I declined politely.

'I'd better not, thanks. The weather's already wild, and we're due more snow.'

In truth, I knew that if I had one, I would drink the rest of the bottle. And then start on someone else's bottle. If I had one, I would leave the car where it was and start the party of the century.

'I'm not drinking,' I confided in a whisper to the girl beside me. 'And I haven't had a drink for a few weeks.'

'Well done,' she said, and she casually took another sip of her prosecco as she turned away.

I wanted to scream back at her. Well bloody done? I don't think you realise what I have just said and how hard it has been! But this was a birthday celebration, not a well-done-Lisa night. I needed to get over myself. I liked to keep my circle small and only had a few close friends. I would confide in them soon enough, but I wasn't in any state to do so just yet. I was too unstable.

I checked my watch. Only forty minutes in. I tried to calculate how long I had to stay before I could leave without appearing rude or upsetting the birthday girl. But I missed my moment.

'Lisa,' someone said. 'If you're driving, would you mind giving me a lift home, please?'

I'd replied before I had time to think.

'Of course I can,' I heard myself say. 'No problem.'

Now I would have to wait until they wanted to go home. Me and my bloody big mouth!

Everyone continued chatting and making jokes. I didn't find any of them interesting or funny, just annoying. Then I felt guilty about my angry thoughts. I focused on the menu, but even the food had booze in it and mentions of red wine gravy and brandy sauce only emphasised my predicament. Was I even allowed to have them? I mean, it was alcohol, right? Could it interfere with my medication? What if I ate some and failed a breathalyser test—how ironic would that be! I was sure I'd read somewhere that the alcohol evaporates when cooked. It was a minefield. Alcohol was everywhere I looked. I tried to enjoy my expensive meal, with its tiny portions in that way expensive meals often are. I swapped the Christmas pudding for the cheesecake. We didn't want to take any chances now, did we?

Once the meal ended, it was party time. Oh, the fucking joys. Everyone was a little tipsy now and the Christmas songs soon started. A few of the gang were up having a boogie, but I sat seething, bitter, twisted and jealous, stewing over my forthcoming shit bag Christmas, and having serious thoughts of grabbing the linen tablecloth with both hands and tugging it as hard as

I could, sending all their fucking drinks flying. Mariah Carey was bleating 'All I Want for Christmas', and all I wanted to do was tear the place apart. I needed some air. I headed to the loo, fearing I was heading towards the point we had talked about in Booze Club, a crisis. All I could see staring back at me in the mirror was venom in my eyes, pure hatred, dark and cloudy, and my skin blazing red with rage. Who was I now? I was turning into a monster. I started crying, staring into the mirror for longer than I should have, and frightening myself. I was going mad. Who was I kidding that I could do this? The craving for drink just wouldn't go away. I dabbed my neck and wrists with cold water and took some deep breaths and looked back up at myself in the mirror.

Stop this. Stop right now. I can do this. I am doing this. I am Lisa Peacock. Get up!

My hands shook as I tried to slow my breathing until I found some strength at last and could compose myself. I topped up my lippy and headed to the bar. Queuing for my Coke, I eyed up the optics and the vibrantly coloured and wonderfully designed glass bottles above them. They had certainly come a long way over the years. I imagined how each one tasted. I once drank a shot out of every bottle of optics behind a bar. 'Doing the top shelf.' Somebody dared me so, obviously, I did. It was easy except for the brandy. I never did care for the stuff. The next morning I couldn't remember anything. Had I done anything stupid? Upset anyone? I would never ever know. That was my first-ever blackout. I was just fourteen, the hero of the housing estate, bigged up for being wild.

'She's up for anything, that Lisa.'

My wild streak made me feel accepted. Looking back, it's no wonder I drank more and more. People praised me for being drunk. Blackouts became a regular occurrence. I thought everyone had them. I woke up in some strange and occasionally dangerous places. Once I was in what I can only describe as a doss house, some sort of squat. I lay on a mattress on the floor, looking at the graffiti daubed on the walls. I had all my clothes on, so I assumed nothing sexual happened. I collected my bag and got out of there as fast as I could.

'Can I help you love?'

I snapped out of my daydream.

'Oh, yes, please...'

I spotted a non-alcoholic cider and ordered one, carrying it back to the table with a pint glass. I felt a little more at ease with the drink in my hand, almost as though I was joining in with the evening's festivities. It looked like a proper pint of booze. I still watched the clock, but I didn't hate the night as much. At one point, I even cracked a smile.

I had half an eye on a group of people on the next table all night. They were in their fifties or sixties and the occasion looked very formal, with straight backs as they ate their meal and chatted. At least, it had been until then. They started strutting their stuff on the dance floor, with jerky knees and elbows in awkward places, hips jutting out in unfamiliar movements. It amazed me how much looser they looked. They were really letting their hair down. *If they hadn't been drinking, would they still be up dancing?* I wondered. They were having the time of their lives.

I also watched my girlfriends laughing and dancing and longed to join them. Over the years, our gang had some amazing nights out. The first one that sprang to mind was when we were running a theatre group. I was the treasurer and in charge of the petty cash tin. Our first play had been an enormous success and we ended up in a club, celebrating. I took the tin to the bar and paid for our drinks, stuffing the receipts in the tin and giggling at how naughty we were being. Miraculously, the tin balanced the next day. We paid every penny back. I suppose you had to be there. Now I wondered if I had lost my wild nights forever.

At the end of the evening a couple of friends climbed into my car, one of them very drunk and slurry. You lucky sod, I thought. Once I'd dropped them all off I was alone, driving in the darkness. Despite my exhaustion, a flicker of light burned within me. I had done it. My first boozy night out. I mean, yes, I had been slightly suicidal and even borderline murderous at one point. It was also a bit shit. But the point was, I did not drink. A smile spread across my face and I had a tear in my eye. After weeks of sadness, tears of happiness finally flowed.

I had never been pulled over by the police. But at this moment I would have loved it. I wanted them to say, 'Can you tell me when your last drink was, madame?' 'Well, actually, officer, it's been a few weeks now...' I would then start a recovery monologue and he would swiftly let me go.

It was at this very point in writing this book that I lost it. Not my mind, the actual book. I was sneakily typing it up at work, only at break times, obviously. But I thought I had cut and pasted it onto my USB stick. I had not. The next morning, I popped the stick into the PC and nothing happened. Where was it? It couldn't be found anywhere. If I didn't save it, then it must be back in its original place on the desktop, right? Nope. I felt an almighty sickly feeling of dread in my stomach, all those words, more than 11,000 of them. It had been pretty emotional going over old ground and now I had lost it all. I phoned my computer wizard brother for help, and he instructed me to bring the stick to his house after work, where he then confirmed that I had never saved my work on it. I burst out crying, ran out of the house and got into my car, sobbing all the way home. Then I did what I do best and ran a bath. A serious mope was in order. I shoved my iPod on shuffle and lay there crying. Who did I think I was, anyway? Writing a book? Pah! People like me don't write books. I'm not good enough. I'm an idiot. How can I be a writer when I can't even save my bloody work? You're stupid, Lisa. Who even wants to read your story? Nobody is interested. You stopped drinking? Wow! So what? Millions of others have done the same. Get over it. All the familiar negative thoughts were with me. You're not good enough. You're not the same as other people. Can't. Won't. Shouldn't. A song came on the iPod that I couldn't remember putting there—*I'm Going to Heaven in a Wheelbarrow* by the Dead South. I sat up and craned my head to the speaker open mouthed. What the hell was that doing there? I had to laugh. And then I cried. And then I laughed and cried at the same time, like a mad woman. The cosmos seemed to send me little messages when I needed them. Something to help me snap out of my doldrums and spur me on. I stood up, like a phoenix rising from the ashes. There I go again, getting ideas above my station. It was just like a woman getting out of the bath. I will write that book, I bloody will! I had worked so hard, gone through nights when I felt suicidal. I felt like I had walked barefoot through fields of broken glass with flamethrowers firing from either side to get where I was. I had seen Satan himself, stared him in the eyes and bitch-slapped him right across his face. I want this to be documented. I want other people to read this and think, If she can, then I can. I know it won't be a bestseller or a coffee table hardback. But if it helps just one person, it will be worth it. Even if every other copy languished in a cardboard box in Mam and Dad's garage for the rest of my life, it will still be my story. My journey of self-discovery. The year I got fixed and found myself again.

Chapter Eleven

Learning to Fly

At the next Tuesday night's Booze Club, the group leader told us a story. Yes, we were all sitting comfortably. Once upon a time, there was an eagle's nest on the top of a mountain. It had four eggs nestled inside, almost ready to hatch, when suddenly an earthquake struck. As the eggs wobbled, one of them fell out of the nest, rolling down the mountainside and landing in a chicken farm below. The chickens set about looking after the egg, taking turns keeping it warm, and eventually, a little bird was born. They nurtured and raised the chick like one of their own. The bird grew into a beautiful, majestic golden eagle. The eagle loved his new family and friends and was grateful they had saved him, but he felt different. He knew he wasn't the same as the others. He couldn't shake off this feeling. His spirit yearned for more. He would watch the skies, envious of other eagles in flight, and thinking, 'Oh, I wish I could soar like those birds.' All the other chickens laughed at him. 'You can't soar,' they said. 'You are a chicken. Chickens do not soar.' But still, he dreamt of a different life. He couldn't accept the one he was living. Eventually, he started practising running and flapping his wings, trying to fly. He tried so many times, and he kept failing, but this didn't deter him. He got back up. He would never give up. Eventually, the eagle did indeed learn to fly. He spread his wings wide and escaped the coop. He freed himself from the shackles of his surroundings and flew through the skies with the other eagles.

The story struck a chord with me. It prised my eyes wide open. I was the eagle, trapped in the coop, weighted down like a battery hen. I just needed to learn to fly, and I will. I'm going to keep getting up, just like he did. Over the weekend, I foolishly told Danny I wanted to get fit and beat my time up Roseberry Topping. He took this as a green light to start an army training camp. I already had an unused gym membership. He got me up at 4.50am. I looked out of the window at the pitch-black road below. I wasn't a morning person. I usually needed at least an hour to crack a smile, more like two hours since I'd stopped drinking. I groggily pulled on some ten-year-old leggings and stepped outside. The icy wind made me wince. Then I saw a rat run from under my car. We lived right next to the river. To me, this was a clear sign I should go back into the flat. The bed would still be warm. But Danny was gazing at me with a huge smile on his face. I didn't want to let him down. He was so motivated. He hit the gym most mornings, while I usually stayed in bed, cozy and warm. Danny never had problems getting up. He had Christmas morning energy every day. Picture a big, happy puppy. Reluctantly, I opened the car door and got in, shivering. The gym was close by, but I hadn't been for so long that the turnstile scanner dobbed me in by refusing to open. I had to go to the main desk and admit I hadn't been for a while. The assistant cheerfully let me know it had actually been over six months, and I had been 'archived' in the system. I felt like telling her exactly what I thought of that. It's five o'clock in the morning and I haven't had a drink for several weeks. Just open this bloody barrier! Instead, I smiled meekly as she buzzed me through. The weights area was no more welcoming, with its floor-to-ceiling mirrors. I looked at myself in the mirror and felt a wave of sadness. I was obese. I was pale. My hair was unbrushed. My t-shirt was a washed-out grey and remnants of last night's mascara were still clogged around my eyes. I had completely let myself go. I didn't want to look like that any more. I struggled to remember the last time I looked into a full-length mirror. I used to be fashion conscious, but as the years passed I stopped caring and spent all my money on booze instead. I would um and ah over the price of a new top but didn't think twice about spending money on wine and cider. Luckily, the gym was quiet. Not many people were stupid enough to be up that early. I didn't have a clue what I was doing, so I was lucky to have Danny with me, my personal trainer, or Sergeant Strongarm, as I now called him. I felt better afterwards. I was glad I made the effort and vowed to make it a regular thing. I even downloaded a calorie-counting app. I had been to many Slimming World groups over the years. I yo-yo dieted and felt too embarrassed to go back and be shamed by my weight gain. I'd wait a few months and then enrol again with a different class. One time I stopped because of an argument with the class leader. Each week you donated a food item for the Slimmer of the Week basket. They were usually low-fat treats—you couldn't just throw a pork pie in. The person who lost the most weight that week won the contents of the basket. I'd spotted a skipping rope in a sale and thought it was a genius idea to give. I popped it into the basket and took my seat. We listened to Brenda talk about how she slipped up eating a pastie and put on two pounds, and then to Maureen, wondering where she'd gone wrong. Linda even told us she gained three pounds because she wasn't eating enough. We finally got to the end of everyone's excuses, and the leader announced the Slimmer of the Week. Then she asked who'd put the skipping rope in. I raised my hand, pretty pleased with myself. But the instructor wasn't laughing.

'You're only supposed to put food in the basket,' she said.

'I just thought it would help with weight loss. Even if you only skipped a bit, just for a laugh, it would be more exercise than you normally would do. Just a bit of fun...'

'You're only supposed to put food in the basket,' she repeated.

Surely skipping was better than eating? Fewer calories! But this woman would not let go. And to be fair, neither would I. She kept repeating the same line, and I kept coming out with positive alternatives. In the end, I suppose I went too far.

'You could always tie the fucking fridge door shut with the skipping rope!' I said.

I didn't go back to that group.

On Saturday I went to the pub, my old haunt. I wasn't sure if it was too early. I would soon find out. The thing was, I enjoyed going to the pub. I loved the banter and the craic. A typical big Saturday in the pub usually consisted of around fifteen pints of cider and a bottle of wine. Not very ladylike, I know. I usually sat with a group of men, as I seemed to get on better with men than I did with women. I put this down to having three brothers. Danny came with me, and I deliberately took the car. As soon as I entered the pub, my rabble saw me. Yay, here's Lisa. One guy stood up and asked what I was having. The look on his face when I ordered a Diet Coke was priceless.

'What, you're not having a drink?' he asked.

I explained I was driving, and he tried to insist I have a drink with them and get a taxi home. Another pal chimed in, also encouraging me to ditch the car and have a pint. I felt tempted. I could smell the atmosphere and almost taste the drinks. But I swiftly came to my senses and realised I just couldn't join in. I said I wasn't drinking at all, that I had decided to stop for a while.

'Behave yourself,' one said.

'Are you taking the piss?' said another.

The entire gang burst out laughing at me, mocking my decision. They didn't think I was serious. I wouldn't get past Christmas. I laughed along with them, but deep down I felt hurt. These people weren't my friends. Not the real kind, anyway. They were just drinking buddies, and I spent no time with them outside of the pub. The bar was a cocoon reserved only for drinking and banter. Somewhere we could forget everything else that was going on in our lives. Now I had left the comfort and safety of the cocoon and stepped out into the real world, where stuff happens and feelings are real. I wasn't in any way better than these people, but I felt I was leaving them behind to venture into a new and better existence.

I now know that it's normal for drinkers to react this way when one of their number breaks away from the pack. They either see nothing wrong in drinking heavily and think you're the fun police and overreacting, or they know they're also drinking too much and dismiss it with ignorance and mocking. I wonder how many of them went home and thought about their drinking that night?

When people asked me why I stopped drinking, I struggled to explain. I couldn't seem to find the right words. The two people in my head were constantly at war over whether I should or shouldn't drink. In the past I would panic if I didn't think I had enough wine to last me until I could buy some more. When I entertained guests I would watch people drinking and mutter curses under my breath. I wanted to shout, 'Stop drinking all my wine!' Drinking was at the centre of my life, the first and most important thing on my mind. My opening question when we went anywhere was, 'Is there a bar?' I couldn't even go on a train journey without alcohol, dressed up in an, 'Ooh look, we're all out and glammed up, let's drink Prosecco on the train' way.

Danny and I were travelling in Turkey when the pandemic began in the spring of 2020. We were drinking on the balcony when we heard some sort of announcement over the mosque's loudspeakers. Not speaking Turkish, we had no idea what they were saying. The next day, as we were about to leave our apartment, our neighbour told us about the lockdown. He explained that only bakers and chemists were open that weekend, to stop the spread of the Coronavirus. It felt like my life was about to become a horror story. But not because the world was facing a pandemic, a disease spreading like wildfire leaving people dead in its wake. No. It wasn't because I was thousands of miles away from my home and worried about my family. It wasn't even because we were trapped in a foreign country with an uncertain future. It was because I had no wine, and I couldn't buy any. Knowing we only had half a bottle of whisky to last us the next two nights that actually made such a devastating event for so many people around the world so catastrophic for me. Pathetic, selfish and ignorant, I started sweating. The whisky wasn't even mine, it was Danny's, and I'd have to ask him for some. My compulsion to drink was overwhelming. There was nothing else to do. Being stuck in that hot apartment would drive me insane. I waited until five in the afternoon, then plucked up the courage to ask Danny if I could have some of his whisky. Thankfully, he said yes, we could share it. I went to get a measuring jug to half it equally but took a quick slug from the bottle before I poured it out. What must he have thought? Right then I didn't care. The sweating and panic were subsiding, as I knew I could get drunk that night. I would have none left for the next night, but I would worry about that in the morning. The whisky wasn't as much as I would have liked, but it was enough to stop me from going into a full-scale panic attack. Later, on the balcony, I tried to ask our neighbour in pidgin English if he could get hold of some wine, or any alcohol at all. I didn't need loo rolls, face masks or hand sanitiser—I needed booze. I tried to explain that we were celebrating Easter, and we got talking. He asked how we would usually celebrate. Embarrassingly, I told him we all bought each other chocolate eggs, our kids had an egg hunt, and then we got drunk because it was a bank holiday and we didn't work on Monday. As it came out of my mouth, I realised how pathetic I sounded. I had just tarnished the central celebration of the Christian religion, reducing it to an excuse to get pissed. Awkwardly, I added that wasn't how all Brits celebrate. But it was how my family did. So that's why I didn't want to drink any more. Because every weekend was like a scene from the movie, The Hangover, where a group of friends wake up after a drinking session in Vegas with no memory of what had happened the night before, and there's a tiger in the bathroom and a baby in the wardrobe. I didn't want the need for a drink to be at the forefront of my mind. I wanted a better life where I was in full control. I had no say when it came to booze. Booze controlled me.

Chapter Twelve

The Road to Recovery

A letter arrived from TV licensing. Apparently, you need a licence to watch BBC iPlayer. I vaguely remembered downloading the police drama Happy Valley, starring Sarah Lancashire. I could have sworn I had a VPN on my tablet, but when I checked, I hadn't paid the subscription. I faced a fine of up to £1,000, as well as any legal fees, even though I only had a crappy ten-inch tablet and no television set. So I came up with a cunning plan. I called the number on the letter and they put me through to a friendly chap named Matthew. I tried to build a rapport by using his name and asking about his day, using my girliest voice and trying to create a connection before delivering him my excuse. This was method-acting at its best. At one point, I even caught myself twirling my hair and pouting.

'The thing is, Matt—you don't mind if I call you Matt, do you? The thing is, Matt, I didn't even realise what I'd done until

I checked my tablet a moment ago. I'm an alcoholic, you see. You do silly things when you're drunk, don't you, Matt?'

I could hear him try to stifle a giggle—my plan was working! I could almost see him smiling. I bet he'd heard some brilliant excuses in his job, but he seemed to like this one. I imagined him being on hands-free and the office all having a laugh. But I didn't care.

'It's OK, I'm getting help now. I haven't had a drink for a few weeks, Matt. Do you think it would be possible to just pay for the programme I downloaded?'

He reassured me and told me not to worry. He would waive any fines and told me to ignore any further letters. He wished me a great day and hung up. I felt triumphant and fist-pumped the air. I promptly deleted the iPlayer app. For once, alcohol had worked in my favour.

I was still feeling smug when I remembered the book I had downloaded. I finally felt I could concentrate enough to read, so I searched for my Kindle. The book was called *The Sober Diaries: How One Woman Stopped Drinking and Started Living*. I didn't expect much, thinking it would be depressing and full of long, complicated words. I prefer easy reads that don't require me to reach for Google or think too hard. However, I was hooked after just a few pages. The author, Claire Pooley, was just like me, although she lived in a more affluent area and had a husband and three kids. She hated herself for drinking, just as I did. She described her cravings as the 'wine witch', which resonated with me because I had my own witch pushing me to drink. I had finally found someone relatable, someone a similar age to me, who understood. I was so engrossed in the book that I forgot about the salmon in the oven. Dry fish for tea, Danny. But it was worth it. I realised there must be thousands of other women out there going through similar struggles. Why didn't I know? Why didn't we all talk about it? I hadn't even known books like this existed. I had found a whole new world I didn't know about—the recovery world. I had moaned on about not getting enough sleep, but now I didn't want to sleep. I wanted to read the book until the end. Would she manage it? How did she cope? It was like she was doing the journey with me. I didn't feel so alone any more. I thought about my own support. I still wasn't speaking to my parents, but my brother Stephen was one of my big supporters. He often checked in on me and asked how I was doing with my recovery. He encouraged me and told me how well I was doing. I considered other people I could reach out to. I had some fabulous friends. But I had to do this by myself. I wanted to prove to myself that I was strong enough to master addiction. 'Self' would be the defining word on this journey of self-discovery.

That night's Booze Club meeting was a good one. It had a less formal atmosphere than usual, and our discussion centred on celebrities who had triumphed over their own addictions. I'll admit to cheating and using Google. I was surprised at the long list of celebrities who had battled addiction, including Pink, Matthew Perry, Russell Brand, Ben Affleck, Bradley Cooper, Elton John and Jamie Lee Curtis. It proved it didn't matter who you were, what you had, or what you had achieved. Addiction was worldwide, and it had no preference. It could affect anyone, regardless of class, wealth, colour or creed. Some felt celebrities had it easy because they were famous and could nip in and out of rehab whenever they wanted. But if I were famous, the relentless pressure would drive me to drink even more. Imagine picking up a newspaper or magazine and being ridiculed because you wore the wrong colour lipstick or gained a few pounds. Having your reputation dragged through the dirt on social media. Always being in the public eye and worrying if you're good enough. Hell, I'm plain old Lisa from Stockton and I felt worthless enough. I wouldn't thank you for being famous. I liked the fact that I could run to the shop in a pair of leggings and not get papped.

They also asked us what logo we would use to describe ourselves. I had no idea what the learning outcome was, but I chose a smiley face. I didn't know why, as I was far from smiley at that moment. But I was a happy person. Or at least I used to be. I wondered if I would ever be truly happy again.

Although my recovery group had been my lifeline, a real-life light at the end of the tunnel, I became frustrated by the lack of support for full-time workers. This was no fault of theirs; they did everything they could. But I sometimes felt I wasn't enough of a drunk. It sounds silly, I know, but that's how I felt. I had somehow kept my job and life in some sort of order. I wasn't entirely sure how I'd managed that. Some days I was so hungover I was merely functioning, my body in robot mode, going through the motions. I would sit in reception, makeup covering the bags under my eyes, and a fake smile plastered on for visitors. But I was dying inside, body and soul. I was fighting waves of sickness, anxiety and thumping headaches. My mental wellbeing was taking a battering. I despised myself for sabotaging my life, but I couldn't stop, which made me hate myself even more. I clung on to a form of normality with an ever-loosening grip. At work, everyone knew me for 'liking a tipple' and being wild, but like so many others, the mask I wore for the world hid a horrible secret, a tale of sadness and despair. If I had lost my job, I would have been able to go to every group that was available. I could have surrounded myself in recovery, like a magic cloak. There was so much on offer—walks, therapy groups, relapse prevention, the list went on. A vast variety of support, but all during the day. I couldn't access any of it because I was at work. I felt passionate about this and made a mental note to do something about it. They talked about an Ambassador course, training to learn more about how to help people with their recovery. All I needed was to be alcohol-free for four months, and I could soon apply. I wanted to learn everything there was to know and completely throw myself into the world of recovery. I had free time in the evenings now. The amount of time and money I had spent on drinking amazed me. Now I needed something else to keep me busy. But when my friend texted and invited me to go Christmas shopping in Newcastle, a nervous pang twisted deep in my guts. Our trips usually involved a few shops, a boozy lunch, a few more shops, cocktails, more shops, and then retiring to a boozer near the train station so we wouldn't get lost when we were drunk and could catch the last train. It was a enormous challenge for me, and I really didn't want to go. But I didn't want to let my friend down either, and I realised I had to get used to normality. Life still went on, and I couldn't hide at home forever. So I replied with a tentative yes, knowing I had a couple more weeks before I needed to think about it. But I had grown in confidence about my recovery. I had turned a small corner. I was only thirty days in, but I felt better in myself and was less emotional. I could breathe a little easier now. I also looked better. I wasn't as tired and exhausted, and my skin looked fresher.

For years I made fun of people, mocked them and teased them, and then I joined them. I ordered myself a pair of leopard print Crocs. I know. I don't know what came over me, I just fancied a pair. Was it time to hang up my cool badge for good? Had I stopped caring about how I looked? No. I just yearned for comfort. I couldn't even excuse it as a drunken purchase. I had made some clever drunk buys in the past. Did you ever hear the eBay notification on your phone and dread even looking? I did that most weekends. During one particularly heavy weekend, Danny and I were in the pub having a Sunday afternoon livener (the only thing that fixed a hangover—more drink), when the eBay bell chimed. I had a quick check and stared at Danny, open-mouthed and wide-eyed. We had only bought a flipping burger van! In fact, not just the van but the whole round too. And it was in London! The grand total of the purchase came to £35,000. I didn't know whether to laugh or cry. What a pair of idiots. We had nothing like that much money in the bank. I don't even like burgers that much. And why London? I had to email the seller and explain I was drunk. He took it well, considering.

Chapter Thirteen

Mourning the Benders

Danny worked hard and rarely went out, so I was happy for him when he said he was going for a drink with some friends. I kept myself busy with my new favourite hobby, reading other people's recovery stories. I had read some fantastic books, including *Sober on a Drunk Planet* by Sean Alexander, *Glorious Rock Bottom* by Bryony Gordon and *Dry* by Augusten Burroughs. Reading other people's recovery stories made me feel less alone. They showed me recovery was possible. People recover, and they were living proof.

I was just lying in bed wondering if Danny was enjoying his night when I heard a loud crash at the front door. I jumped out of bed to find him sliding down the door frame as he tried to jiggle his key into the lock, and I helped him inside. He stumbled around and slurred his words, telling me he loved me. I could have punched him. He tumbled onto the bed, still dressed and reeking of booze. When the snoring started, I snatched my pillow and headed for the living room where I lay on the sofa, staring up at the ceiling with tears streaming down my face. I was angry and upset, and not entirely sure why. I suppose I was jealous that he got drunk and had a good time. I was also annoyed that he wouldn't be desperate to do it again tomorrow, and envious I didn't have that option. But how could I be mad at him? He worked more than sixty hours every week, supporting me and not having a drink for weeks to cheer me on. No wonder he needed a blowout. I knew I wasn't the only one going through all of this. Danny had to deal with it too. He didn't ask for any of it but never complained once and stuck firmly by my side. The next morning, I took him a cup of tea, a bottle of water and two paracetamol. I sat on the bed next to him, the stench of alcohol turning my stomach and making me queasy.

'I felt a bit miffed last night,' I admitted. 'You were so drunk you couldn't walk or talk properly. Was there any need to get that drunk?'

Danny sat up straight and looked me dead in the eye, amazed I would say such a thing. 'Well, you needn't talk…'

Then he noticed the glint in my eyes and realised I was joking. We both burst out laughing. We really needed to laugh more. Now that I had got over the harrowing ordeal of detox, I could joke about my recovery. It was the only way I knew. I've always said, no matter how shit life gets, no matter what happens, you can strip me of everything, but you can never take away my sense of humour and ability to laugh. Nobody can steal my laughter. I left him to sleep it off and went shopping.

Elton John came on the car radio, singing *I'm Still Standing*, and the lyrics felt so poignant, especially knowing what he had also been through. When the chorus came I felt a tremendous rush of joy, happiness and achievement. I was looking like a true survivor. I burst into tears, but they were happy tears. I felt joyous, hopeful and positive. I was doing it, and I was still upright. I was getting on top of it. Surviving. Right then, I also felt like a little kid. For the first time, I thought, *Yes, I can do this*. I was full of fight. It felt like the beginning of something. My elation soon turned to sadness, but more for the ordeal I had gone through, not just detox, but the years of being lost and drunk. I didn't realise just how broken I had been. When you are in the thick forest of addiction, you can't see the wood for the trees. I didn't realise how far I had fallen. I had become trapped in an endless cycle of self-harm. But not any more. I was fixing myself. I was going to beat this, and I was going to have the best life from now on. I would make sure of it. I felt like dark clouds were parting and the thinnest shaft of light was forcing itself through. It's tiny, but it's a start, and I'm clinging on to it. Better days were coming, I could feel it. I wiped away my tears and got on with the shopping, humming the song as I threw food in the trolley, with a fresh spring in my step. I hurried around, eager to get home. I had a man there who needed a cooked breakfast. I burst into the flat, unable to wait to tell Danny. I jumped on the bed and shook him awake, talking so fast he had to calm me down. I told him all about the song and how I felt different. I was turning a corner.

'I can do it, Danny. I know I can.'

Things were going to get better. Even with his fuzzy head, he was laughing at me, so pleased for me. For us.

Chapter Fourteen

A Journey of Firsts

My friend asked me to look after her cats at her house. She lived in a beautiful cottage a stone's throw from the sea. I called it my beach retreat. Going there always felt like a little holiday. I loved watching the waves from the dining-room window. From the bedroom, you could see the cliffs of Saltburn. I was still drinking the last time I had house-sat for her. I had planned yoga on the beach, walks along the shore and an evening of pampering and reading. It hadn't quite turned out like that. I ended up in the pub by eleven in the morning and started a one-woman pub crawl. I sat with various older men I had never met before, betting on horses and drinking pint after pint of cider. They belly-laughed at my jokes all day, saying I was hilarious, for a woman. Cheeky buggers. One said he had never known a bird who could drink so much. Pubs were my safe place. I had never felt self-conscious walking into a pub on my own. In fact, I enjoyed going to a pub by myself. I made more friends when I was flying solo. Mam once said I could make friends in an empty house, and she was right. I enjoyed their company for most of the day and bought a bottle of wine on the way home. I was so drunk I struggled to climb the steep stairs and I felt so ill the next day that I was too scared to drive home. Danny had to jump on a train to collect me and drive my car. He wasn't happy. But this time would be different.

I arrived in the late evening, treated myself to a zero per cent glass of wine and attempted an early night. I had no sleep in me. I lay staring at the ceiling with the window open, listening to the waves. I would love to live near the sea. After just a few hours' sleep, I dressed and made my way into town. I entered an amusement arcade where the sounds and smells reminded me of my childhood. The flashing machines played nursery rhymes, and candy floss and sugar dummies surrounded the change kiosk. I changed some pound coins into two pence pieces and stood for a long time, feeding them into the machines. It felt like an escape from my real world, spending the price of a night out drinking pints of cider to win a 20p keyring. Mam told me that when I was a kid, they would put notes in the change machine. When the change fell out of the bottom, they would pretend I'd hit the jackpot and say, 'Look, Lisa, you've won!' Damn tricksters. I treated myself to a bag of chips with scraps and made my way to a bench, where I sat watching the dog walkers. I wonder what they'll be drinking later? A glass of wine or a G&T? I'd become obsessed with guessing what other people drink. Once I had decided, I then got angry that they were having a drink and I wasn't. I couldn't think of anything else. Booze was still at the forefront of my mind every day. I fed my last few chips to the seagulls and headed back to the house, grabbing myself an ice cream on the way home, a 99 with a flake, nuts and raspberry sauce. No sooner had I walked away from the kiosk than the wind whipped up and I got ice cream and sauce in my hair and all over my face. I couldn't stop laughing. People were looking at me because I was roaring so loud. Today was a good day. Yes, I thought about drink, but I didn't have one. I had fun without it. I realised this journey was all about firsts. The first time in a pub, the first celebration, the first night out. One step at a time. I would go through every single one until no more firsts remained.

I didn't have long to wait until my next big first—my first sober shopping trip, scheduled for the following weekend. I was nervous all week as the big day loomed. The only light relief came when my Crocs arrived, delivered to work. I giggled as I opened the package. These weren't any ordinary clogs. The leopard print design and zebra strap saw to that. I figured if I was going to wear silly shoes, I needed to go bold, and bold they were. They were the comfiest thing I had ever put on my feet. Tiny little nobbles inside gave me a massage as I walked around the office. I did a few catwalk twirls and even received a couple of wolf whistles. I loved them. I could have kicked myself for not buying them earlier. That night I ordered a second pair, fur-lined no less.

The morning arrived and I carefully picked out my outfit and spent extra time on my makeup. Walking to the train station,

I felt good. I had no thick head. I wasn't hungover. I wasn't rushing and I looked forward to spending time with my friend. We met on the platform and she told me how well I looked, giving my ego a little boost. We boarded the train to Newcastle and I started telling her a little about me giving up drinking. I played it down, not mentioning how my life had been hell for the last few weeks. She was shocked and kept saying, 'I can't believe it,' but she also said how proud she was of me. I heard her say the word 'proud,' but I didn't listen. I had always been bad at taking compliments and focused on how I'd got myself into the mess. Like when I had lost weight—'Wow well done you, you look amazing.' What for? Neglecting myself and piling on weight only to have to work hard to lose it again? It felt like a double-edged sword.

By now I had £500 in my no-drink savings and decided to treat myself. I was on the lookout for something shiny. I had seen a beautiful ring online and started searching for the shop. We made a pit stop in the first pub. My friend ordered a G&T and then looked guilty.

'Do you mind me having a drink?'

'No, don't worry, it's fine,' I said.

I ordered an alcohol-free cider, and my friend insisted on paying. The price shocked her.

'But there's no booze in it,' she said.

I laughed. Welcome to my world.

We had a fantastic day. I thought about drinking, but I didn't have one. I didn't find my shiny new ring either, instead treating myself to a vintage beret and some face creams. I couldn't bring myself to dip into my no-drink savings. I didn't want to break the figure, as it matched the days I hadn't drunk. My sober streak.

We headed for the train and found the carriages packed out, with no seats available. I stood, clutching the handrail. With all the bodies crammed together, the heat was stifling. I took my coat off, and then it started. Panic. I could feel myself struggling to swallow and gasping for breath. All around me was a blur. I was frightened to say anything. I couldn't think straight. What was happening to me? The train was pulling into Sunderland.

'I need to get off,' I told my friend. We were only one stop into our journey home. But the station was freezing, and the air cooled me down. I felt so stupid. I apologised profusely.

'I thought I was going to have a full-on panic attack.'

I hadn't had one for over fifteen years. My wonderful day out had now left me feeling deflated. The next train wasn't due for fifty minutes, so we walked around until we found a pub. I ordered a Coke and my friend had a G&T. I felt guilty. I sat down and looked around. We must have picked the roughest pub in Sunderland. People with teeth missing and red-faced, bloated old men stared at us like we were fresh meat. Men older than my dad, the creeps. I could have murdered a large wine. I was so upset about the train. If I had been drinking, I wouldn't have felt that panic. I would have been too busy laughing and planning our drinks for when we got off at the other end. The next train was even busier than the last one. I didn't even step aboard. I apologised again and promised to pay for a taxi home. My friend was understanding and told me everything was all right, but I knew I was being a pain in the arse and wished I was better. We headed to another pub to order a taxi, but I called Danny first, and he collected us. Not only had I spoiled my friend's day, but now I'd also ruined Danny's. I'd passed the shopping test but failed to cross the finish line. But I was still taking this day as a positive step forward in my recovery. I would try my best not to dwell on what went wrong, but on what I had achieved. I had faced a massive claustrophobia incident, but I didn't turn to drink. I could have strolled to the pub and ordered a large Jack Daniels to settle my nerves, but I didn't. It was a vicious curveball, but I dodged it. All right, I didn't get on the train. But I had found another route home. And I suppose that's what recovery is about. Finding out what works for you.

Chapter Fifteen

A Stubborn Standoff

Christmas loomed, and I still hadn't heard from my parents. We were all being stubborn, but there were two of them and only one of me. They must have discussed it and decided not to get in touch. So I dug my heels in. Were they embarrassed about me? Alongside dealing with recovery, the fallout was constantly at the back of my mind. I missed them, but they had hurt me. Maybe I had overreacted, but my feelings counted too. Other family members pressured me to offer an olive branch, but I questioned why I should. This was the biggest fallout I had ever experienced with my parents, and it mattered to me, even if they didn't realise it. Yes, my emotions were running high and I had erupted, but it hurt me they hadn't come to check on me, given the challenge I was facing. However, I didn't want any drama to jeopardise my recovery. I was doing well now, and it had taken me over twenty years to get to this point. I wanted them to be proud of me, but they didn't understand the severity of my addiction, and I was too exhausted to explain. We usually visited my parents for Christmas lunch, but this year I'd spend time with Jimi, and Danny and I would have the rest of the day at home. The chef at work kindly offered to plate me two lunches, and I couldn't resist her offer. It felt a bit rubbish cooking Christmas dinner for just the two of us. I feared a visit from the Ghost of Christmas Past. Memories of previous dramatic Christmases flooded my mind—sleeping in for lunch, giving the wrong presents, vomiting throughout the day, blackouts, heartburn and even a trip to A&E one year. I didn't want any of that drama, of course, but I longed for the fun side—laughing with my brothers, pulling crackers and teasing Dad about his dad jokes. I wasn't sure if I would ever experience that again. Would I always have to watch other people enjoy themselves? An outsider looking through the window into the fun house? What a depressing thought.

Work was busy, with dutiful relatives visiting their loved ones for Christmas. But I had already grown tired of it all. With strict visiting guidelines in place, the reception element of my job had taken over from the admin tasks. I was sick to the back teeth of hearing the words 'Covid' and 'stay safe'. I knew they were in place to protect the vulnerable, but some rules seemed plain stupid. Let me give you a few examples, without using the real names. John Smith was a resident in our care home, admitted under the end-of-life category. This poor man had come to us to die. He was lovely, and I sat with him when he arrived. He was such a charismatic and funny guy, telling me tales of his RAF past and how his career as an engineer had taken him to many countries. He even shared the story of tasting pink champagne for the first time on a trip to Poland and giggled like a schoolboy as the memories flooded back. He mentioned he liked a tipple of G&T, and his son was bringing him some that afternoon. However, the care home rules dictated they must keep anything brought in a 'safe' holding room for forty-eight hours to rid them of Covid germs. 'But this man is dying,' I told my colleagues. If he wanted a bloody drink, surely he could have one. It might have been his last one. I made an executive decision and bought two cans of ready-mixed gin and tonic from the nearest off-licence and smuggled them into the home. I put on gloves and anti-bacterial-wiped them to within an inch of their life. Another chap ran out of cigarettes, but when a relative delivered emergency supplies, they had to stay in the quarantine room for two days. It felt like I was banging my head against a brick wall. The cigarette packets were nonporous, wipeable products, and we could easily glove up and wipe them down. Meanwhile, the poor man was gasping for a fag and having withdrawal symptoms and screaming at staff and residents.

When they told us in a staff meeting that we couldn't wear Christmas jumpers and reindeer ears, as we usually did, I finally lost the will to live. What the hell is the point of that? I muttered under my breath. I mean, where was the logic? The answer I got was we couldn't wash jumpers in water hot enough to kill any lingering Covid germs.

'How do you know I wash my uniform at a high temperature?' I asked. 'Or even at all, for that matter? It was an incredibly tiring time. The care home had to obey strict guidelines. Of course they did, I fully understood that. But I was frustrated. We were all having a rough ride. We just wanted to go back to normal and I felt so sorry for our residents. They didn't let us put up Christmas decorations either, and these poor people hadn't even seen a smile for months, just faces with masks on. Then there was all the red tape. We were all forced to have the vaccine. The residents living in our home had the choice, but the staff had that right taken away. I didn't mind. I wanted to do what I could to stop the spread and protect our residents. But why did some people have more human rights than others? One girl had a strong allergic reaction to inoculations and was terrified of the vaccine. Besides worrying about her own health, she also had two small children to think of. She loved her job, which was all she had known since she started working, and she held off getting vaccinated as long as she possibly could, but eventually had no choice. She had to be vaccinated in a controlled clinical setting because the risk of seizure was so high. I was dumbfounded by the experience she had to go through. We were wearing masks and full PPE—there must have been another way? I agreed we should do what we could to protect vulnerable people, but these residents were approaching the final stages of their lives. I don't mean they didn't matter as much. But knowing hospital staff didn't have to vaccinate, even those bringing new life into this world, running neonatal and intensive care units, left a bitter taste with care home staff. These poor girls didn't get to stay home on furlough payments, they worked twelve-hour shifts on the minimum wage to keep our care homes running. They arrived for work not knowing how many residents would die that day or if they would get infected and put their own families at risk. All in a day's work? They all deserved medals for bravery!

I was busier than ever, but it became monotonous, Covid-testing visitors and escorting them around the building, while trying to keep on top of my work. I felt ready for something new, something different. I upgraded my CV and monitored the job market.

I opened a text message from my best friend. She was inviting me to a Party in the Park event, a 1990s' dance event playing all the old music from when we used to go clubbing years ago. The familiar pangs of anxiety churned up my stomach. But not wanting to let her down, I typed out YES and pushed the send button. Then the panic set in. How would I go through a whole festival without drink or drugs? At least I had some time to get my head around it. That night in Booze Club we talked about radical acceptance, something I had never heard of before. It was about accepting what is out of your control and embracing what is happening now, without judgment. Fully and radically accepting emotional or physical pain can reduce the suffering it causes. It took me a while to understand. I suppose it was just too, well, radical. When I first thought about things that upset me or people who hurt me, accepting it felt like forgiveness, but it's not. Did I cling onto the hurt and feel pain, unable to get over it when a previous boyfriend cheated on me (true story)? Such pain causes damage inside, stopping me from trusting someone else, being happy and moving on. At some point, we just need to accept facts and draw a line in the sand. Why let the past ruin your future? Someone once told me, 'If the past comes knocking at your door, don't open it. It has nothing new to say.' I have never heard anything so true. I had mulled over the past and clung on to the trauma, but it was time to stop and move on. The therapists may not phrase it precisely like this, but shit happens. We talk about it and get over it. They also discussed the importance of learning to accept the hand we are dealt. That way we can move beyond the pain of the past. We flourish in the present and look forward to the future. If we held our hands together, palms upwards, we could register that we were accepting something. I gave it a go the next morning, starting small. A car cut me off on my way to work, the driver signalling obscenities as he passed. I felt tempted to chase him down like a dog, but instead, I pulled into a lay-by. I sat with palms together and accepted that he was a dickhead, and I wouldn't let it spoil the rest of my drive or my day. It felt good. I wasn't sure if it would help with the bigger challenges life would throw at me, but it wouldn't hurt to try. Anything for a quiet life.

The Zoom meetings were informative and helpful, but I needed something else. I wanted to hear other people's stories, how they had recovered and what their coping strategies were. Weekends were especially difficult and I needed extra support.

An idea started swirling around in my head—always a dangerous prospect. I thought it might be good to start a recovery group on WhatsApp, where we could reach out when we felt alone or struggling. I wasn't sure it was a good idea or even if I would be allowed to give out my phone number. But I went for it anyway. I asked permission from the facilitator and asked what the other guys thought. They agreed it was a fantastic idea, so I shared my number. I was concerned I would get tons of messages, but I could just mute the alerts and check when it suited me. By the time I went to bed that night I'd had three requests. It was starting. I added them and creatively named the group 'CGL Gang'. 'Booze Club' might be too blunt for some! I added a slogan: 'I stopped waiting for the light at the end of the tunnel and lit that bitch up myself.'

In the days that followed we discussed some basic rules. Nobody messaged anyone directly, only through the group. We only met in groups of three to keep ourselves safe. And what happened in CGL Gang stayed in CGL Gang—a bit like Fight Club but without the booze and the violence. I started the ball rolling with just a few details—about my addiction and how long I had been sober. The others soon chipped in, and it felt like the start of something new, another outlet for my recovery. Knowing support was always with me was a breakthrough.

Meanwhile, I tried to keep busy organising Christmas, making sure I had a gift for everyone. I was unsure what to do about my parents. Should I get them a gift, or was that two-faced? Why would you give a gift to someone you hadn't spoken to for weeks? But they were still my mam and dad, and I loved and missed them. I was just too stubborn to admit it—I must have inherited that trait from them.

I decorated our little flat and added a small tree. It was only two feet tall, but it was all we needed. The smell reminded me of driving through the pine tree-lined, windy roads of Switzerland, the branches all dusted with snow. Despite the freezing temperatures, it had been a stunning sight. Nothing a camera could pick up, more of a feeling. That 2019 trip taught me how kind so much of the world is. Sadly, the pandemic put a halt to our travels. We returned home but stored our plans safely on the back burner for another day.

Four days before Christmas, I heard my phone ping. It was a text from my dad, asking if I was going to their house for Christmas dinner. Unsure how I felt about the invitation, I read it out to Danny. Yes, it was a short and sweet, get-to-the-point message, but it was still an olive branch, he said, and I should accept it. It was what I had been waiting for, for weeks. I replied telling him we already had Christmas Day plans, but we would pop round in the morning to exchange gifts. And then I put it all to the back of my mind. I would think about it later.

I was at work on Christmas Eve and planned to take a festive drinks trolley around the home to share a tipple with the nanas, as I called them. I was supposed to say residents, but it just wouldn't stick. I had done it the previous year and in that short time it had become a tradition and was expected of me. But this time was going to be difficult. I had started telling work colleagues I was stopping drinking for a year. You know, mainly to lose weight. Just a personal challenge. When the day came I cleared my desk, donned my illicit reindeer-antler headband, and started my trolley. I lined the base with wrapping paper and added plenty of tinsel. I had a wide range of seasonal delights—mince pies, panettone, yule log, lebkuchen, Christmas cake, crisps, nuts and pretzels. But the top shelf was where it was all happening. Sherry, brandy, whisky, wine, prosecco, gin, rum, bucks' fizz, lager and beer. On the end was a lone imposter, a bottle of Nozeco. All the other bottles laughed at it, but that was for me. I pressed play and the festive tunes started as I pushed my treat cart to the first unit, dancing to Wham's Last Christmas. The nanas loved it. Those who could got up and did a little jig, while those who couldn't danced in their chairs. It was lovely to see them laughing, although I had to stop Molly from having her third whisky, the little tinker. I moved to the next unit, where my entry song was Slade's *Merry Xmas Everybody*. This was a nursing unit, so many of our clients were in bed.

I walked into the next room and a lady was sitting up in bed as Bing Crosby sang about *Silver Bells*. I introduced myself and showed the lady the delights of my trolley. When she saw the cake, her eyes widened like a child's on Christmas morning. I handed her a slice and sat beside her on the bed while she ate her cake and sipped her shandy. She was so happy. She lived in a care home, stuck in her bed and rarely had a single visitor. And yet her beautiful smile lit up the room. She made my day. We should all take a leaf out of her book, I thought. I needed to work on what I should be thankful for. I had complained and moped around because I couldn't drink, but I was alive and well. That should have been enough.

Chapter Sixteen

Christmas without the Spirit

My first Christmas Day without booze arrived. No champagne with breakfast, no sherry after lunch and no countless glasses of wine for the rest of the day. But I could do it. Danny and I kissed and wished each other Merry Christmas, then invited the dog on the bed for cuddles. Because we found Jesus as a stray, we didn't know how old he was or when his birthday was. We decided that with a name like his, today would be a fitting day to celebrate. After exchanging gifts and singing 'Happy Birthday, dear Jesus', we went for a long walk along the river.

Outside was much busier than I had expected, and we got talking to a man who was sitting alone on a bench. Most of his family had passed away, he told us, and he found Christmas hard. He had too much time off work to think about his loneliness. I offered him my reindeer antlers, thinking they might cheer him up, but he declined. We chatted for a while before going our separate ways. I held Danny's muscular arm a little tighter as we walked on, knowing how lucky I was to have people who loved me around. And here I was, ignoring my parents for weeks.

We climbed into the car, but it didn't feel right. Danny seemed to have the ability to read my thoughts. We both looked at each other, me with tears in my eyes. Seconds later we were on our way back to find our guy and offer him dinner. I would give him mine, and Danny would share his with me. We got back out of the car and split up to cover ground quicker. We searched for forty minutes but couldn't find him. We tried our best.

After that we headed to my parents' house. My insides leapt around with nerves. We could barely look each other in the eye, but we plodded on. We never spoke about our fight, we didn't mention my alcohol-free journey and we didn't exchange any apologies. That's how my family works. We don't talk about things. We never have. We just brush the past under the carpet and move on, leaving wounds unhealed. It felt like my recovery wasn't important. I wanted to scream out: 'Look at me! See what I'm doing and how bloody hard it is! I'm working my socks off to make changes. I'm trying to get over a problem I've had for what feels like my entire life. I'm trying to better myself. I'm struggling. I need your help!' Instead, I kept quiet and smiled. We didn't stay long, but it was enough to break the ice and I arranged to visit again the following week. I was glad I had seen them and relaxed a little.

We couldn't fit a dining table in our small flat, but today we had put up the camping table and chairs. I dressed it with a tablecloth and candles. It was a far cry from all those perfect Christmas dinner table Facebook posts, but it was enough for us. I swapped my champagne for a flute of apple juice. My shoulders sagged at the thought. But hey—it was only one year. Next Christmas would be different. I would treat myself to something special.

On Boxing Day, my friends and I reserved a table at a local pub. Various friend groups joined us throughout the day. I've always loved Boxing Day. It's a chance to wash away the stress of Christmas. There's always pressure to have the perfect Christmas Day and it can all just get too much. But this year was going to be different. Usually, the day involved heavy drinking for me, but I was going to abstain. Instead of indulging in multiple pints, a few proseccos and then a bottle of wine with Danny when I got home, I opted for a non-alcoholic cider. It's only one Boxing Day out of seventy or so, I told myself. I needed to remember everything I'd learnt from the guy on the bench we met the previous day and the lovely nana at the care home.

Everyone was dolled up and a couple commented on how well I was looking. I thanked them politely. Liars, I thought. Nobody noticed I wasn't drinking, but I noticed they were.

As the afternoon went on, my cravings for a drink became stronger. Seeing everyone around me indulging made it even more challenging. On our table was prosecco, rosé, white wine, gin and tonic, brandy and Coke and a pint of lager. I could easily have downed every single one, one after another, even the brandy. The force was strong today and the cravings were hitting me hard. I had the car so I couldn't drink, but it didn't stop me from wanting one. The atmosphere was bouncing, but I just wasn't feeling it. I couldn't wait to go home, sleep and start a new day. The experts say take it one step at a time, but this step was icy, slippery and embedded with six-inch nails. I was sick of not being able to drink, sick of thinking about drink and sick of watching people drink. One girl was getting more drunk by the minute and getting on my nerves repeating herself and saying stupid comments. By the early evening my frustration became too much. I made an excuse and stepped outside to call Danny. I needed to vent, and regrettably, he was on the receiving end. He reassured me about how well I had done so far. The feelings will pass, he said. Go and enjoy the company of friends you haven't seen in a while. That was easier said than done. I knew he was right, though. I came back in with a fresh perspective. *I'm Lisa Peacock and I can do this.* Soon I was joining in the fun as we joked about finding an eligible man for a single friend.

For the first time in my adult life, I didn't feel ill or hungover on December 27th. I didn't wake up watching the clock for when I could have my next drink. I didn't worry if I'd made a fool of myself. I was up, ready and excited about the day ahead. I took advantage by climbing Roseberry Topping with the dog again. It was still challenging, with a few moments where I had to catch my breath, but it was certainly easier than before. I reached the white-capped summit and checked my watch. To my delight, I had completed the climb in sixty-eight minutes, beating my previous time by seven minutes. A small improvement, maybe, but it was progress. Little steps, my friends.

We joined our old friends and spent New Year's Eve at a caravan park. We had lived in a small caravan on the site for twelve months while we were saving money for our road trip and made some lifelong friends there, especially Dawn and Andy, a couple who came from Doncaster but were contracting up here in the North-East. Their little caravan was a cheaper alternative to local digs. We hit it off right from the start, and every minute spent together was full of laughter. They lived on the opposite side of the field to us, but later moved across and we became neighbours. We spent a lot of time together; meals out, walking and barbecuing outside our vans. Even their dog, Lexi, accepted us as one of the family and would often wait outside our van for us returning from work. It was an amazing experience and a time I will never forget, but not without its challenges. The caravan was tiny and cold, the water pipe would often freeze and we had to walk to the washing up bay every night. When the wind blew the entire caravan swayed and rocked. But living there brought a sense of liberation. We brushed our teeth overlooking the Cleveland Hills and star-gazed while eating our tea. We saved a lot of money, even though I also spent most in the on-site pub. I treated the place like my front room. But this time when I arrived, everyone knew I wasn't drinking, and a few mocked me. I joined in with the craic. I'll spend £5 maximum, drive home, and be fighting fit in the morning, I thought. You, my friends, will be at least £150 down, stumbling home, most likely being sick and stinking in the morning. Cheers! I raised my Coke to that. The pub was packed, and a sweep across the tables confirmed I was the only person not drinking out of the hundred or more in there. Stopping drinking wasn't just a personal challenge. Socialising also posed a struggle. I was a tiny stickleback swimming against the hungry pikes in a big pond. People just assumed I would drink, as if we were programmed to booze at every opportunity. The urges weren't as strong as they had been on Boxing Day, although I could merrily have sunk a glass of fizz at midnight. But as we counted down to the New Year, I gripped my Coke. Danny and I were close, and we gazed into each other's eyes. Another year together. What new adventures would this one bring? He told me how proud he was of me, and that he loved me. A tear dripped down my face, smearing my mascara. In all my years, I had only heard 'I'm proud of you' about three times. No doubt I had made people proud, but hearing those words out loud felt special. I was also proud of myself. I looked around and saw everyone drinking while I went against the grain, the only sober one. Then the round of hugs, handshakes and kisses began, as we wished each other all the best. One guy slurred a few words as he kissed my cheek, but I couldn't make out what he was saying. He reeked of booze. I felt repulsed. At that point, I wouldn't have thanked you for a drink. I sat in silence, collecting my thoughts, while the rest of the pub sang and cheered for the New Year. I cheered inside for myself. I hadn't had a drink for sixty-one days. That was at least 120 bottles of wine. Wow! Here I was on New Year's Eve with a Coke. Look what I'd done. Little old me. I had realised the severity of my problem, I wanted to change, and I did. I bloody well did. It had been a painful journey so far. It had almost broken me, but I was getting stronger by the day and things were changing for the better.

Chapter Seventeen

New Year, New Job

In the first Booze Club of the new year, we talked about something I had never heard of before—self-soothing. We discussed what made us feel better when we were down. Once a month, during my period, I felt like the worst person in the world. A bath and listening to Radiohead usually sorted me out. We were told to think about putting together a self-soothe box we could take out during especially difficult times. I started mine off with a candle, chocolate, a cooling eye mask, photos of happy memories and people I loved and two lists. One was the positive changes I'd made since I stopped drinking. The second was the goals I still wanted to achieve. Learning about self-love and care made me realise how much I had neglected myself over the years. That was going to stop. From now on, I would put myself first.

As January progressed, I focused on going to the gym and getting fit. I jumped on the scales and saw I'd lost nineteen pounds in total. I was dumbfounded. This never happened to me. I couldn't believe it. For years, my weight had fluctuated thanks to yo-yo dieting, but now I could lose weight for good, since I wasn't consuming half of my calories from wine. I smiled at myself in the mirror, breathed in and puffed out my chest. My skin looked clearer and less red, my eyes were bright and my hair had a glossy sheen. All the pain and hard work was finally paying off. I had forgotten I could feel this good. I vowed to stick to my weight-loss and fitness programme.

I now qualified to undertake the Programme at Recovery Connections, which was the next step from Change Grow Live. It would mean being part of the solution for other people with addiction issues as a visible role model, supporting their recovery during a six-week course. I downloaded and completed the form during my lunch break. I needed references, so I asked a friend and Danny's mam. An excited thrill surged through my body. The course could be a springboard to a new career. And it could teach me new things about my own recovery. I soon came back down to earth. They introduced a new pay scale at work and every employee had received a pay rise—but my increase was the lowest. I immediately fired off an email to HR. A running joke in the care home went that it could function without a manager but not without an administrator. I wasn't laughing. My pay should have reflected my contribution as part of the management team. This was just the push I needed. I downloaded the Indeed app and found a job in another care home. The position and hours were identical to my current job, but the pay was better. I didn't want to go into another care setting career but needs must. Within an hour, I had received the offer of an interview that same day. As soon as lunchtime came I rushed home, put on some makeup, curled my hair and grabbed some heels. The new place looked like a stately home. This just felt so right. I sat in the car and waited for a few moments, taking some deep breaths. I think my calmness was because everything was happening so quickly I didn't have time to overthink it. I knew I was going to get the job. After all, after twelve years in the job I could do it with my eyes closed. My confidence and capability must have come across in the interview because they offered me the position on the spot. I called Danny and we met in our favourite Italian restaurant. I emailed my resignation between forkfuls of delicious carbonara.

Even after the buzz of a new job, I woke up the next morning feeling low. Everything around me seemed muted. I wasn't living, just existing. Alone. Was life really worth the agony? Would I feel like this for the rest of my existence? Days had turned into weeks, but everything still seemed black and white, lacking vibrancy. An endless, pointless cycle—gym, work, don't drink, sleep, repeat. I needed another outlet, something beyond the weekly Booze Club calls. I had the idea of creating an Instagram page to document my progress. Keeping it private seemed like the right choice. I would never show my face or mention my real name. I was still ashamed of being an alcoholic. Society makes you feel ashamed. People were shocked and sometimes looked disgusted that I became addicted to one of the most addictive substances in the world.

Danny loved the idea. We brainstormed for a page name, but all the obvious ones were taken. Eventually, I settled on nodrinkforme. Fortunately, it was available, so I set up the page to claim the name before someone else took it. The next challenge was figuring out what to upload. Sharing every moment of my life online wasn't me. Too showy. As an Instagram novice and technophobe, I depended on Danny to show me the ropes. My first post was a screenshot of my counter app, showing fifteen weeks had passed without drinking. Then I waited nervously for a response. I only received five likes, but knowing five people had looked at my story and were happy for me meant a lot. Five people were interested in my recovery.

Curiosity led me to an internet search for alcohol-free, sober and recovery-related content. The results opened my eyes. So many people around the world were coming together. Recovery was the one thing they had in common. One big recovery meeting, right there on my phone in my pocket. I could finally express how I felt on this platform, and other people would get it. I started following a few people, and they followed me back. My recovery family began to grow. I was building support.

My colleagues made a display for my last day at work. A huge board was placed in the entrance, with lots of little love heart notes and a photo of me in the middle. I blushed at the lovely things people had written about me. My manager had even written a poem.

Cat wrangler, cashing up mangler.

Prone to dog rescue, Jesus will tell you.
Super crier, teetotal trier.
She tells us when she needs a poo, you know, as you do.
Danny lover, Jimbo's muvver,
I don't think we'll find another, like you.

At the top of the display, large letters spelt out the words, 'Our rainbow'. The thoughtfulness of my friends and colleagues touched me deeply. After saying my goodbyes, and crying a few tears, I gathered my belongings and packed them into the car, before taking one last look back. I'd had some happy times here. And right here in this car park would always be where I started my recovery journey. But I knew I couldn't go back. From now on, I would only move forward. A tear trickled down my face as I waved goodbye to our stray cat, Tiger.

As I drove to my new job the next morning, Glaswegian singer Gerry Cinnamon came on the radio singing about today being the beginning of the rest of your life because time is running out. A rush of exhilaration swept through my body. This was the beginning of the rest of my life. I could feel it now. Despite the challenge I still faced, I started to perceive a glimmer of hope ahead. For the first time in years, I could think straight. At forty-three years old, I knew I was running out of time. Gerry was right—life should be a canter. It's amazing how quickly your emotions can change. Last night, everything was hopeless, and now I was looking towards the future with genuine hope. I was on a crazy, yo-yo trip, spinning up and down between highs and lows.

I was just about to step into my new workplace when an email arrived. Recovery Connections had accepted me for the course. But my elation soon turned to deflation. The dates and times were all during the day while I was at work. It must have been a mistake. Later, after my first shift, I called the number to check. But there was no mistake. Another opportunity slipped away from me because I worked. I would have to use my annual leave to attend any classes. The course was all I had thought about for weeks, keeping me going during my darkest moments. I knew it wasn't their fault. They had so many groups running and they couldn't cater for everyone. After crying for what felt like forever on Danny's shoulder, I made a decision. I fired up my laptop and found an online counselling course at a nearby college. This would be another first for me. A proper qualification.

Chapter Eighteen

Back in the Rat Race

The weekend was here and the highlight was a 1990s dance festival. I danced around to club classics all morning as I got myself ready. I chose my outfit and was getting into the party spirit. And then it started. At first my hands shook as I tried to apply my makeup. Then my heart began thumping and the room was spinning around me. I gasped for breath. I couldn't cope with this. I remembered these awful feelings all too well. I had once been so anxious that I was off work for three months. Panic attacks became my everyday normal life, and I struggled to leave the house. It was happening again. Crippling anxiety. I called my friend and through my tears I tried to explain I wasn't well. I knew I was letting her down, as there were only two of us going. She said she knew a couple of other friends who were going and I told her to meet them. I would join her later. I took some calming medication and tried to rest. Waking up feeling a little better, I continued getting ready.

Loud dance music was pumping out as I arrived at the gig, transporting me back thirty years when I would tour clubs around the country. That time was messy. Drinking and drug-taking, heavy weekends that took me all week to get over. Before I'd even entered the grounds I was already thinking of just having half a cider to take the edge off my jumpiness. Or maybe a little bump of cocaine. This was a dangerous place for me to be. Still, I carried on through the turnstiles and looked for my friend. I found her in a tent watching singer Alex P and tried my best to get into the party mood. I could feel the sweat running down the back of my neck in the sweltering heat. Everyone around me had either a can of cider or lager in their hand, and many were gurning, a telltale sign they had taken drugs. I knew they were just trying to loosen up, reminisce and have fun. But some of them were embarrassing. Fifty-odd-year-old women with glitter on their faces, trying to relive their youth in a tent at two o'clock in the afternoon. I wasn't judging them. I'm not like that. It's their life and they could choose what they want to do with it. But this just wasn't who I was any more. I loved the music, but I didn't want to drink or take drugs. I was alone in a sea of 6,000 people. I felt like I was the only one who wasn't on something, and the only one not having fun. I was a fool to have come here. It was too soon. A chocoholic wouldn't go to Thorntons for the day, so why the bloody hell did I think I could come here? All so I didn't let my friend down. With my tail between my legs, I made my way back home.

For the next week, anxiety surrounded me like a shroud. I had a holiday planned and was worried sick I would feel like this while I was away. My palpitations were the worst I had ever had. I was fighting off daily panic attacks and just getting up to go to work was a battle. I was exhausted and terrified. Last time this had happened it had lasted for months, and I feared history was repeating itself. The doctor prescribed the beta-blocker propranolol. That weekend taught me two valuable lessons. One, dance music was a major trigger for me. But more importantly, I would never put misplaced loyalty or anyone else before my recovery ever again. I come first. My recovery is my priority.

My next social event, a few weeks later, helped take my mind off my worries. After getting ready, I laughed out loud as I tossed a Capri Sun into my handbag. Just a few months earlier it would have been half a bottle of vodka in my bra. Oh, how my life had changed. My friends and I were going to see Paloma Faith at the Globe Theatre and we met up at a bar in town for pre-gig drinks. We hadn't seen enough of each other since the pandemic. We continued having a good old gossip as we headed arm in arm to the venue. Only when I handed my bag over to the security staff to be searched did I remember the Capri Sun.

'What do we have here?' he said, pulling the squelchy sachet out.

'It's a Capri Sun, sir.'

He grinned.

'You didn't intend to drink that inside the venue, did you?'

'Don't be so silly—I wouldn't do such a terrible thing.'

He winked and told me to get lost. I tottered off inside, packing the contraband back into its hiding place.

I loved the show. I'm not the world's biggest Paloma Faith fan and only knew a couple of songs, but as well as being good at what she does, she was also funny. She had genuine charm. What made the night special for me, though, was how she opened up about her own vulnerabilities. She told us she lacked confidence and would go home and pick at what she had done wrong with her performance. It's good to share these things. We sometimes assume famous people have it made, but they aren't a different species with no feelings. They are everyday people like you and me, but with exceptional pressure on them to perform. Life is rarely easy, is it?

We don't always realise the importance of engaging in meaningful activity. In Booze Club, we talked about a 1970s' experiment where a scientist placed some rats into a large cage along with two water bottles, one of which was laced with opiates. The rats all killed themselves by drinking the drugged water. But the scientists decided the experiment was unfair, as it didn't reflect real life. There were no other distractions, and human lives didn't work like that. So they built a new, bigger cage and filled it with all kinds of distractions such as food, toys and wheels to keep the rats occupied. They discovered that the rats that socialised, ate the food and played with the toys only took occasional sips of the drug-infused water. The rats that didn't play or socialise drank the most from the opioid water and soon became addicted. I suppose the loner rats had nothing better to do. Our lives should be full of meaningful activities. Otherwise, what's the point? On reflection, I had built myself a fun rat park after I stopped drinking. I learned new skills, changed my job, joined a gym and filled my hangover-free weekends with activities. The first recovery book I read said addicts are often creative people. So had I become an alcoholic because I was bored?

The Booze Club WhatsApp group was a godsend. One girl told us she'd had a terrible day and the worst was yet to come, a friend's hen party. Her concern wasn't about drinking, but about the constant pressure to have one. Even the bride-to-be wanted her to toast her special celebration. How would she cope with all the questioning? Why aren't you drinking? Can't you just have one? What, don't you drink at all? Never? She was going to sound ridiculous. But it wasn't ridiculous; it happened to us all the time. I used many excuses when people quizzed me. I sometimes didn't want to talk about the real reason. I'm on antibiotics. I'm driving. I don't fancy one. I have to be up early in the morning. Wasn't it pathetic that I couldn't just say I wasn't drinking that night without the Gestapo getting the thumbscrews out to start the interrogation?

'Fancy a ciggy?'

'No thanks, I don't smoke.'

Completely acceptable.

'Fancy a pint?'

'No thanks, I don't drink.'

'We'll just have one, maybe just a small one or a shot. Try it. We'll have a laugh. Go on!'

We live in a drunken world. The response one time when I casually mentioned I didn't drink was comical. People wrinkled their faces up in disgust and let their mouths drop open in mock horror.

'You're boring, you are.'

I recalled nights when I would have replied, 'Behave,' and drank the lot of them under the table. I could match any man, pint for pint. I didn't need to do that now, though. I just smiled politely and thought about how fresh I would feel in the morning and how much cash I would still have in the bank. In truth, my life used to be boring. How mundane, to sit in a pub week after week, spending all my money on drink, only to go back to work on Monday feeling like crap and recover just in time to repeat the cycle the following weekend. Like a drunken hamster wheel. My life was full now. I didn't have time to sit wasting a day in the pub. I had far better things to do. But this poor girl in the WhatsApp group cancelled her day out. The pressure was just too much. Instead, she sat at home alone and got drunk. She relapsed because of society's pressure to drink. What was wrong with people? I could have cried. Why couldn't we just respect each other's decisions to live the way they wanted to? Sadly, people with addiction issues face these hurdles every day, and trying to explain to people is a constant challenge. They didn't understand. How could they? Without our support she would have faced this alone, but at least she had us. The group was worth its weight in gold. We tried to reassure her that we all face bumps in the road, but it was pointless to dwell on our mistakes—we had to learn from them. It's what happens next that really matters.

Chapter Nineteen

Crete expectations

My holiday was coming up and I still felt anxious after the rave episode. It had rocked my confidence and made me question whether I was strong enough to see my recovery journey to the end. I always felt like I was fighting a war, up against some sort of barrier or challenge. I needed a bloody suit of armour! But that's what makes us stronger—seeing barriers and learning to overcome them. After a couple of weeks on the prescribed medication, I started feeling a little better, no longer fearing I was about to have a heart attack. But the next battle was starting. I was excited about going to Crete to visit James and Catherine, friends who we met while travelling in 2019. We had parked up on a beach in Turkey and I noticed their British number plate and headed straight over to introduce myself. That night, we drank wine, chatted about anything and everything, and formed a bond. We didn't know it but we would spend the next three months locked down in Turkey together.

Covid took a terrible toll on the world, but I'm lucky to say I had a positive experience and met some friends for life.

I hadn't flown for three years and the whole airport experience terrified me. Airports and drinking had always gone hand in hand. I had never flown without a belly full of wine. The minute we arrived at the airport my knees started knocking in fear. I followed Danny through the double doors. Among the sandwiches and croissants in the small coffee shop, I spotted a bottle of Magners cider. It stood tall and inviting and promised calm and relaxation, condensation dripping down the sides of the glass. We don't sell drugs with the morning papers, so why sell booze in a coffee shop? I could taste the cider in my mouth and imagine it trickling down my throat. Just one bottle would stop me from feeling so anxious and dull my senses just enough to get me through this. How else would I manage? Instead, I walked back outside for some air and took a photo of the airport sign for my Instagram page. 'First flight sober,' I wrote. I told Danny I was struggling and as soon as it was out in the open, I felt a little more settled. We found a sofa out of the way and held hands while we both read. Super cute. The response on my Instagram astonished me. People sent messages of encouragement, and some contacted me privately to offer their help. Strangers from thousands of miles away took time out of their day to support me. They could have just scrolled on by but they stopped, took notice and tried to help. Recovery is a community where we lean on each other. These strangers got it. They knew exactly how I felt. They've been through the same. All were at different points in their recovery, but experts nonetheless. One of my followers even shared my 'soberversary' date. We checked up on each other now and then, and when she asked for advice it made me feel I was good at something, a thread in the beautiful weave of the recovery tapestry. I knew I could seek help any time of the day. Instagram is magical. Because it's global, there's always someone online somewhere in the world. I never knew when the cravings were going to hit or when I might need to tap into a resource. Having my virtual allies behind me gave me the strength I desperately needed.

We made our way through security before finding two free seats close to the bar. A sign on the wall proclaimed, 'Drinking is fun'. Once I would have agreed, but now I could see how pathetic it is. I sat people-watching—men with swollen bellies drinking pint after pint, ladies opting for a wine or a G&T. They couldn't get enough of it. I was seeing every aspect of my life differently. I didn't think I was better than anyone else. Far from it. But I did feel like I had joined an elite gang. Like I knew this secret that others didn't. I was part of a mighty movement, people who were choosing to live differently, going against the norms of our society. I started relaxing but also felt a little silly, all that worry and angst for nothing. This was another test, and a big one, but I was coming through. My knuckles were white. As we headed for the gate, the tension go to me. Fortunately, my GP had given me some diazepam, my flying pills. I popped a couple and soon I was settled. Take me to Crete!

A beautiful shade of blue skies greeted us and I felt good. James and Catherine's house was in a stunning location overlooking the coastal village of Almyrida. This was just what I needed. Spending time with our friends was wonderful. Although we had only known each other a few years, we had become close. It's hard to explain, but I admired them and felt safe around them. Their company was just so easy. I had been reading Victoria Hislop's The Island, which documents life on the Cretan town of Plaka, home to a now abandoned colony of people with leprosy. Our friends took us on a mini road trip to the island in their beautiful motorhome. With perfect timing, I powered to the end of my book on the eve of our trip. The book was so fresh in my mind I could visualise everything the characters had described. I savoured the atmosphere and imagined what life would have been like for them. I felt so lucky to have such an experience and soaked up every second. This experience would have been wasted on me when I was drinking. I would have rushed across the island to the end to get to the bar for drinks by the water's edge on the other side. Life was different now. It felt good. Positive, healthy and meaningful.

Later in the day we headed for the beach nearest to where we were camping and picked a trendy bar to loaf around in. James relaxed and read while I lay sipping my minty, syrupy, alcohol-free mojito, looking over the ocean onto Spinalonga. Catherine and Danny splashed in the sea, trying to persuade one of her dogs to swim. I could hear laughter all around me and the gentle sea breeze refreshed my face while the sun warmed my body. I wanted to frame and keep this moment forever. I realised I wasn't 'going without'. This wasn't me struggling with cravings. I wasn't winging it. This was happening. This was real. This was recovery. This was me having fun on holiday without drinking. I could do this and I was doing it. A feeling of deep joy washed over me and I felt a tear slide down from underneath my sunglasses. I was rebuilding my life, piecing together each fragment like a jigsaw puzzle of my body and mind. Some pieces were snapped or scuffed and needed a little glue to hold them together, and some had lost their bright colours. But I would work on myself to bring those vivid colours back to life. I could now look to the future and see my life without alcohol, where I didn't need to drink because life itself was enough. I had spent so many years on this earth but was missing its beauty and wonder. I was here but not present. My mind was too focused on drinking to soak up moments like these. We spent the rest of the week sightseeing and dining out. I felt the odd pang of a craving, but I was okay with that. My friend let me sniff her wine. It stank, and the cravings passed. I looked a little odd, but whatever worked—this was my recovery.

Ten blissful days later, the time came to head home. I admit I had a tear in my eye after the perfect holiday. I knew I would miss my friends, but I left with memories that will last a lifetime.

Chapter Twenty

Making the Connection

My support worker had been talking about a permanent move from CGL to Recovery Connections. We all started off with CGL, and once we completed our dialectical behaviour therapy (DBT) course and were alcohol free they encouraged us to move on to a different type of support—aftercare, if you like. I was apprehensive about losing the help and camaraderie of the regular Zoom meetings. How would I bridge the gap? What if I fell off the wagon? What if I couldn't cope on my own?

After weeks of complaining about our local Recovery Connections' lack of service for me, they called to tell me they had set up a face-to-face group for full-time workers and would meet on Thursday evenings—starting that night. I was buzzing. At last, I could meet other people in person and not on a screen. I also felt I had been listened to. I was sure I was far from the only person needing after-work help, and my constant bleating had helped to make it happen. I changed my plans to make sure I could be there.

The meeting was everything I'd hoped it would be and just what I needed. We were a small group, but I loved meeting people from different walks of life and listening to their stories and experiences. One girl explained how she had been in a controlling relationship in which her boyfriend plied her with drinks. Eventually, she was hooked, and he had her where he wanted her. After months of abuse, she escaped his clutches, fleeing with only a carrier bag of belongings and her faithful dog. She was gradually rebuilding her confidence and taking control of her addiction — what a fighter.

Another guy told how a traumatic incident in his life led him to drinking. When he drank, he forgot. I suppose we can enter a safe world when we are drunk and avoid facing the harsher realities of life. Another girl had recently had her child taken away by social services because of her drinking. She said it would be so easy to just pick up a drink and get obliterated, as she felt her life was already over. The very worst had already happened, so the outlook couldn't get any darker. My heart went out to her. And I agreed; life couldn't get any worse. I couldn't even imagine how she felt, yet she was still here, still battling to get her head above water and take a breath. I leaned over and whispered to her.

'It can't get any worse, but it could get better. Surely the only way is up now.'

I listened to all the different stories of how people started depending on alcohol. I could see through tiny windows into their lives as they shared their journeys so far. Nobody was prying or judging. We chose what we wanted to share. All very different people, we wouldn't have met in our usual worlds, but we all shared something in common, and it brought us together. We were all at different stages of recovery. Some were just approaching detox. In other cases they had been drug-free or dry for weeks, months or even years. It didn't matter if we used alcohol or drugs, we all learned from each other. Sharing our stories was liberating, and I felt included. I was no longer surviving on my own. It was real and raw, with no stigma or pity. Meeting so many real people from my own community made me realise how prevalent addiction is. I didn't want the meeting to end. I had finally found my people, my tribe. It felt like reuniting with long-lost friends. I felt a positive rush and a renewed motivation to do more for my recovery and help others.

I picked up some leaflets as we said our goodbyes, and I closed the door behind me. One of the leaflets mentioned a 'Writing for Wellness' session, which intrigued me. Writing and documenting my recovery in words and the odd poem had been helpful, and I wanted to learn more from an actual author.

When I got home, I stuck the leaflet to my fridge. I could think about that later. For now, I turned to Facebook for more recovery support. I searched for Recovery Connections and found various events, but they were all during the day when I was at work. Despite the frustration, I eventually discovered a wellness walk nearby on Saturday morning. I messaged them and arranged to meet. I brought Jesus for support; animals can be an excellent distraction technique. I stood outside, waiting for the others, but only two guys showed up. One also had a dog. Initially, the atmosphere was awkward, since we didn't know each other. However, our dogs seemed to get along, even though his dog kept trying to lick my dog's tinker throughout the walk. Which was embarrassing. Never work with animals or children. We started talking about our addictions, and I shared that mine was alcohol, while the others struggled with drugs and alcohol. We discussed the challenges of navigating our lives without substances and the difficulty of adjusting our social circles. One guy asked if I was a believer, but I wasn't certain what he meant until he prompted me further.

'You know,' he said. 'God.'

The crucifix tattoo on his face should have been a giveaway that he had turned to a higher being for help. I had thought it was just a trendy inking.

'I don't *not* believe,' I said.

I don't judge anyone who believes in God. Several people have mentioned the Twelve Steps to me, but I have been hesitant to explore it because it sounds somewhat centred around a higher power. However, I do like the idea of having something tangible to celebrate each achievement, like a shiny token for each sober milestone. We all find strength and guidance in different ways. Religion just isn't something that resonates with me. Not yet, anyway. But who knows? I'm open to trying new things.

'I'm an alcoholic, in recovery...'

There. I finally said it out loud. A girl at work was asking questions about why I didn't drink. A colleague being interested in what I had to say somehow made it easier. I told her I had been a client at Change Grow Live and then Recovery Connections, and that I attended weekly meetings. Then we swapped questions and answers. 'Why did you start?' 'How much did you drink?' 'What was the turning point?' Another two members of staff walked in, but I just carried on talking. The floodgates were open, and once I started, I just couldn't stop. I had an audience, and I was on fire. I tried to explain why I had kept quiet until now and how I felt shameful. And then I burst out crying. I think they were tears of relief. My colleagues were intrigued, in a positive way. They wanted to learn, and I was their teacher. We all agreed that we don't talk about alcoholism enough. Most people have a stereotype in mind and I didn't fit that idea. Heavy drinking was pretty common where we all lived and getting drunk every night was a regular event for many people and accepted as normal behaviour. But I found myself being congratulated and told how proud I should be of my achievement. It was only then that I realised how far I had come. I had put the last twenty-odd years behind me and begun rebuilding my life in a matter of months. I'd had to look deep inside my being and change who I was. I had reinvented Lisa.

I sometimes called it a rebirth because it was an opportunity to start living my life. But I didn't realise how many layers my recovery had until I started peeling them away. I imagined each recovery layer as a coat, and I was wearing so many they weighed my body down. I couldn't concentrate on my life or wellbeing because of the burden of these heavy coats holding me down wherever I went. I Imagined the coats had labels on them—embarrassment, worry, cravings, failure, self-neglect, lack of confidence—the list could go on. One at a time, I was shrugging the coats off, and each time I did so, my load felt a little lighter. But it was challenging. I struggled with what I found underneath each coat and had to work on it. Sometimes I wanted to put one coat back on. I felt vulnerable and didn't know who I was any more. I had forgotten who I had been before the addiction took over me. What were my values? What was really important to me? What did I do before drinking? I suppose I had drunk from such an early age that I never got to know the real me. Now I was finally growing up and finding out who I was. I didn't even know what clothes I wanted to wear any more. This was my chance to completely reinvent myself. I was no longer the person I had been when I was drinking. I could control what happened to me now, not just stumble along with no aims or goals, letting life pass me by. I started this journey thinking it would be for twelve months, and for the first six months I believed it, constantly counting down the days until I could have a drink. But over time, something changed. I was eight months sober and my life had evolved. I had a feeling of wellness and positivity. Would I want to introduce drinking back into my life? Did I even want to? Sometimes, I picked a glass of wine up and considered what would happen if I took a drink. Sometimes I willed myself to take a sip. But deep down, I didn't want it. It would poison my life again and I had only just cleansed it.

Friends and colleagues often asked me if I would ever drink again. The answer was no, I wouldn't thank you for a drink. It would never be just one drink. It would come with lots of baggage for me, far more negatives than positives. But how could I live the rest of my life without a drink? Where was the fun? My life changed in so many ways and I found joy in different places. Everything was just better—forests smelled fresher, waterfalls were clearer and the sunrise was more beautiful, with promises of new beginnings and possibilities every day. Sunsets were calmer and more peaceful. For the first time in years, I felt in charge. I controlled my future, and I could achieve what I wanted. The toughest part was deciding what fabulous thing to do next. I went from wanting to stay at home, comfortable in my safe place where I could drink without judgement, to throwing myself at life. Danny once told me, 'Comfort is a cage.' I got it now. I had locked myself away in a cell, with hangovers and anxiety keeping me imprisoned. Now I had found the key and escaped. My raging thirst for adventure was back. I wrote poetry, went axe-throwing, shooting, hiking and swimming in lakes. I loved trying anything different. What used to look like mountains to me are now minor hurdles. All I needed was a plan to get over them. Drinking wouldn't bring anything to my life. I wasn't missing anything for it to fill.

Chapter Twenty-One

Seizing my Second Chance

I was sad when the time came to attend my final Booze Club Zoom meeting and leave my recovery gang. I had my Thursday night meetings now and hoped they would be enough for me. I constantly worried about losing my way. I listened to everyone else talking and waited patiently until the end to announce that it was my last time. We promised to keep in touch via our WhatsApp group, and I encouraged them to share my number with any new people joining the Zoom meetings. Afterwards, I lay on my bed to gauge how I felt. I was no longer scared. It felt like a positive move, another rung on my recovery ladder. I was climbing higher.

Later, I searched the saying, to 'fall off the wagon' and discovered it dated back to the Prohibition era in 1920s' and '30s'

America. The men who worked on the wagons used to clean the streets swore an oath to remain without alcohol and be 'on the water wagon'. People later shortened this to simply being on the wagon. In the past, if I wanted to know anything, I would have to go to the library and read a book. Those days were long gone. Now, with the internet, I could ask Google questions every day. It's amazing how accessible everything had become, including finding a partner through Tinder without leaving the house. I'd found out all about those mystery jars I'd found in the spice rack. Sassafras came from North America and is popular in creole and Cajun cooking. I discovered that galangal is used in Vietnamese soups and Thai curries. It was all news to me. And I still had no clue why they would be in my cupboard. The internet had even made alcohol become more accessible, with the existence of services like the Moonshine van that delivers alcohol, mixers and cigarettes where I lived. They list their prices on social media and accept debit and credit cards. There's also a Dial-a-Balloon service that delivers balloons and nitrous oxide canisters, although I'm not sure if that's quite so popular.

I woke up the next morning on a fluffy pink cloud. After a 5am gym workout, I drove to work while singing along to *You Shook Me All Night Long* by AC/DC. It's amazing how much music can influence your mood. I think I had stopped listening, trundling along with the radio on but not caring what the DJ played. Now, I had a world of music at my fingertips thanks to Spotify, and I made the most of it, meticulously selecting my playlists. Just as I was pulling off the motorway, a beautiful rainbow appeared in the sky above me. I burst out crying, obviously! You couldn't write this stuff. I felt blessed and the magic of the moment made me smile even wider. Years ago, I would have scarcely noticed—it certainly wouldn't have given me the same rush. Little rushes of happiness and joy now filled my life. Euphoria. I was through the darkness. I felt changed. I only saw light. Where I was once so negative, I only looked for positives now. For years, I hadn't been living; I was just existing in a mundane rat race. Now I could see clearly. My eyes were wide open. I was seeing the world for the first time. I wanted to soak up everything life could offer. I had never felt so motivated. This was my second chance.

One of the most exciting opportunities that came my way was the Writing for Wellness group. I was so keen to join and meet the author, Helen, that I took a half a day's annual leave. It was for women only, and there were just four of us. Helen introduced herself and started telling us a little about her career and writing. She had worked in social care for many years, alongside the police and various charities, but she had left this career to focus on her writing. She explained how writing had helped her through her grief when she lost her beloved grandma. She even had her book published and had since supported many women and found writing had also helped them. I told her how my scribbles had helped me out of some dark places and she suggested I should put them together to write a book.

'People like me don't write books,' I said.

Her response was instant.

'You have a story to tell. You can write a book.'

In truth, I had been mulling over the idea of making the notes I had been writing into a recovery memoir, but worried I wouldn't be good enough or that nobody would be interested. But this lady told me I could. She said I was an inspiration. I had never thought about myself like that before. It made me proud and emotional. Once again, I was trying to hold back tears. Helen's supportive nudge of reassurance was just what I needed. We talked about other avenues of writing and how we might even make money from it. Did you know some magazines would pay £25 just for an inspirational quote? I've been wracking my brains for one ever since! Other avenues included daily gratitude notes, postcards, letter writing and journaling. She explained how journaling could be less pressure than keeping a diary. It didn't matter if you missed a few days. We chatted about how we rarely wrote letters anymore, and I told them about the love notes I sometimes sneaked into Danny's lunchbox. We all had a good laugh about that.

Helen challenged us to write down a few things we were grateful for. One of the other ladies said she was grateful for joining today's group and that she had met me. Wow! Her honesty took me aback and touched me deeply. Being surrounded by people who openly discussed their feelings was incredibly refreshing. People had said such lovely things to me lately. I wasn't used to it. I had always been an emotional person, but since I'd stopped drinking, I found it even harder to control my emotions. I used to think people just said nice things to me to be polite, but why would they? I was starting to believe them, and I needed to give myself more credit. I was always kind to others but never kind enough to myself. Women, on the whole, are like that. We can be our own worst enemies. When somebody said my hair was nice, instead of just replying, 'Thank you', I would say, 'Yeah, I've just washed it.' When somebody said my dress is lovely I would say, 'What? This old thing? It was only cheap.' Why did we do that? From now on, I was going to try to just accept the compliment. I left the group feeling inspired and motivated. I would put all my notes together and get them typed up. It couldn't hurt to try!

Chapter Twenty-Two

Jesus Loves You!

A young girl told me my Crocs were the trendiest she had ever seen after I was brazen enough to walk to the local shop in them. Why had I even doubted myself? I knew they were cool. I couldn't wait to tell Danny. Okay, she also said they reminded her of Bet Lynch, but he doesn't need to know that bit. On the way home, I took time to sit and reflect on a bench by the river. I was proud of myself for telling my colleagues what was happening in my life. It had probably spread like wildfire throughout the workforce now, but I didn't mind. Maybe I should climb up onto the rooftops and start shouting. It could help someone else. Sharing my secret was a major step forward in my recovery and I couldn't wait to discuss it with the group. I had met many people who were unabashedly open about their recovery and used to think how brave they were. They must have been so confident to just put it out there. And now, here I was, getting more confident by the day. I returned home and posted a picture of a bottle of alcohol-free rum on Instagram.

Alcohol-free drinks helped me so much. At the start, they were the only thing that made me feel part of a group of friends while socialising and helped me join in. I didn't drink them that much now, only at gatherings. I also realised they weren't for everyone and could even be a trigger. Someone thought it was a brilliant idea to leave a negative comment on my post.

'Drinking that is like swapping seats on a crashing aeroplane or switching rooms on the Titanic.' Now, I'm all for freedom of speech, but was that necessary? I slammed the phone down onto the table. Everyone's recovery is different, tailor-made for their personality. What works for one doesn't work for another. We're supposed to be supportive, not to mock each other. I wouldn't dream of making a negative comment to somebody in recovery. Or to anybody for that matter. I would just scroll past if I didn't like what I saw. I couldn't seem to let it go and kept thinking of clever and witty remarks to reply with. I wondered if he would have said that if we were face to face, or was it a classic case of a keyboard warrior? What a prick! The only way I could find to let it go was to delete his comment and press unfollow. I could have argued with him all day, but I had bigger issues to deal with.

Putting on my bra the next morning, I felt something on my back, like a scab that was hanging off. Danny had gone to work, so he couldn't look at it for me. I decided to leave it alone and got ready for work. I was sure I had a mole there, and I thought the top of the mole must have come off, although I couldn't understand why.

As I drove to work, I convinced myself I probably had skin cancer. I had seen things on social media where moles changed colour or became crusty, and it almost always turned out to be cancer. After months of battling my addiction, now this! I had just read a book about a woman who stopped drinking and then got breast cancer. She still didn't drink, but I wasn't sure if I could stay sober if I got such scary news.

As soon as I got to work, I asked Joe, the maintenance man, to look at my mole. He was a good friend, and we got along well. Our connection was there from the first day we met. Despite being several years older than me, we were on the same wavelength—silly and down to earth. He told me I didn't have a mole, just a scab, and called me an idiot. I demanded that he take a photo. It turned out I had my sides mixed up, and the mole was on the other side of my back. I inspected the photo, zoomed in to the affected area, and finally saw it clearly. A tick. A dirty tick. I recognised it because I had pulled ticks off my dog before. I felt sick and knew I needed to get it out right away. At that moment, the chef heard me screaming and rushed into my office. I begged him to remove the tick, and he came back with his best knife. I ended up lying on top of my desk while the maintenance man shone a torch on the crime scene and the chef carved the tick out. What a moment for my manager to walk in! It resembled a scene from an old Carry-On film! She simply shook her head.

'I won't even ask,' she muttered, and she left to make her morning coffee.

The chef removed as much of the tick as possible but announced he may have left a stray leg behind. I felt like I was going to vomit. I rushed to my doctor's surgery, giving them a courtesy call on my way. The GP was a kind lady. Until she brought out the needle, at which point her sadistic streak came out. I had both hands on the wall as she dug in and scraped away the last leg. The pain was searing, making me feel queasy. She prescribed antibiotics and sent me on my way.

I finished the course of antibiotics, but after a few weeks I still didn't feel well. I can only describe it as like having soup for brains. I couldn't concentrate, was forgetful and constantly tired, like a foggy hangover. Something felt very wrong, so I called the GP's surgery. I had to wait in a queue of ten people but secured a 9.50am appointment. I was so forgetful I had to write my symptoms down. On the drive to the doctors, I convinced myself I might have had alcohol-induced Korsakoff dementia because of years of heavy drinking. The thought crossed my mind that if I were diagnosed with dementia, I would probably start drinking again. Then I remembered Ronnie Wood of the Rolling Stones, who had consumed enough booze over the years to sink a battleship, but still fathered twin girls when he was almost seventy! I really needed to work on my tendency to overthink. The doctor took my bloods and told me to drink more water, then sent me back to work.

I woke up the next morning feeling very unwell again. My head ached and I had a sore throat and raging earache, but I dragged myself up and got to work. An hour later I had to go home. I hated being off work and unwell, so I moped around the house for two days. I picked up a little, but I still felt low. I had hit a slump. For the last couple of months, my glass had been half full, and now it had evaporated altogether until only the dregs remained at the bottom. I had hit a wall, and worried my sober streak was over. I had done so well since my detox. I was motivated and had grown as a person. The only way was up, it seemed. But now I was feeling glum and went in search of anything I could find to cheer me up and ate three Cornettos in a row. But my craving wasn't for sugar, it was for booze, and it rocked me. It was months since I stopped drinking. Will someone please turn this shit off! What more did I need to do? I was exhausted.

Danny returned home, and I blurted it all out—how fed up I was with fighting addiction. I just felt like giving in. I knew it wasn't the answer, but it was how I felt. As usual, Danny came up trumps. He told me to pack a bag—we were going camping.

My migraine returned as I sat in my camping chair. I was restless and wound-up, for no other reason than wanting a drink. I took Jesus for a long walk. The sun blazed and I was grateful for a gentle breeze on my face as we found a spot to sit down. I hugged my knees to my chest and watched the stalks of corn swirl around, painting patterns on the fields. I took it all in and took a deep breath, feeling sad. Would it be like this forever? Fighting an addiction that would always try to creep back into my life? Choosing all over again to live a sober life, every single day, especially when I was surrounded by drinkers, was draining. Tears streamed down my cheeks once more as the dog nestled in, gently nudging me with his long nose, reassuring me that everything was all right. He'd had such a terrible start in life—living rough, eating out of bins, sleeping in abandoned ruins and staying alive through the harsh Bulgarian winter. Even after everything he went through, he never lost his faith in us humans. He never gave up. He knew I was sad and he wanted me to be happy. He was a bloody inspiration. I had a stern word with myself and headed back to camp with a fresh outlook on my life. Later, I watched the sun go down as I sipped my alcohol-free rum and ginger, with my faithful dog at my feet and holding hands with my handsome man.

Chapter Twenty-Three

Ticked off

We decided to move house after our neighbour finally drove us to the edge. Listening to a forty-five-minute loop of Celine Dion belting out *My Heart Will Go On* hammered the final nail in the coffin. I was sad because I loved our location, just a stone's throw from the River Tees. We could wave at the early morning paddlers as we worked on our truck at the waterside, and we often fed the swans and watched the sunset on our bench. I say our bench because I had once fancified it up, adding potted plants on either side, making a seat cushion and dressing the ironwork with bunting. It lasted five weeks before somebody stole the planters. I came back fighting and glued two more pots down with Sticks Like Sh*t adhesive. They lasted a whole eight weeks. Friends often commented on how lovely it was. When the sun shone—which admittedly wasn't that often in our part of the North-East of England—it felt almost like being on holiday.

After a long search, I found a property I loved, and would you believe it, it faced the river. Just a mile away from our current home, it was a mews house with two bedrooms. It was perfect. Our front garden merged with the riverbank path, where we had often walked with the dog. We had an extra bedroom, and the gardens were low maintenance. A couple of days before the planned move I had packed as much as I could in preparation, cramming Lizzy the Nana-mobile to within an inch of its life. That was what we called my seventeen-year-old Clio, with its red paintwork and vintage cream interior. It was exactly the kind of car someone's grannie would drive, so the name just stuck. The move went without a hitch and we clocked up 25,000 steps in a day, carrying wardrobes, fridges and bloody Land Rover parts! We were already a very happy couple, but I knew we were going to thrive and cherish this house.

On our first night in, I had an almighty craving to drink. We had moved house many times, and it seemed like a tradition to order takeaway food and christen the new home with some bubbles. But there was no champagne that evening. We did indeed order a takeaway, but I toasted our new home with alcohol-free rum and lemonade. When we woke up the next morning, I looked out of the window to see the sun beaming on us. I couldn't conceal my delight as we sat outside and enjoyed breakfast in our garden. After living in a tiny flat for over a year, it felt like finding treasure.

Later, I went shopping and noticed a new drink product on the supermarket shelves. Infused with CBD, they promised to help you relax, reset and reduce stress. 'Take a moment for yourself' the packaging urged. I mulled over the decision while wandering through the aisles. They didn't contain any alcohol, so I wouldn't be drinking, but they did have something that would alter my state of mind. After my usual overthinking, I decided to give it a try and put four cans in my trolley. Once home and done unpacking, I grabbed one from the fridge and poured it into a wine glass with ice and a sprig of mint. The aroma reminded me of a mojito. I sat on the sofa, staring at the drink and drumming my fingers on the arm of the chair. I raised the glass to my lips, but something didn't feel right. I shared my concerns with Danny, who agreed it might be an unwise move. I didn't need anything to make me feel different. I swiftly poured the drink down the sink and gave away the rest of the cans. I understood the importance of not replacing one addiction with another. In my search for a kick I had often found solace in shopping for pre-loved clothes on Vinted. Finding the perfect bargain gave me a temporary boost, but I slowly realised it didn't fulfill me in the long run. I didn't need to chase a high any more. I deleted the app and resolved to fill my life with meaningful activities instead.

It had been a challenging week as I battled symptoms including a racing heart, dizziness, tiredness, sweating and sleeplessness. I've been in a cranky mood every day. After researching online, I concluded I was going through menopause, despite being only forty-four. Didn't I have enough on my plate? It seemed as though someone had a voodoo doll and relentlessly jabbed it from all sides whenever things were going smoothly for me. Concentration became difficult, and I even forgot what I was saying mid-sentence. It felt as if I was starting my detox process all over again. Exhausted, irritable and desperate for rest, I prayed to anyone who could hear me for a full night's sleep and vowed to contact my doctor the next day to ask about hormone replacement therapy. I made a mental note that if I ever got the chance of coming back to earth, I was not coming back as a woman, and definitely not an alcoholic one.

When the surgery number came up on my mobile phone at work the next morning, I joked they must be psychic. I'd been spending a lot of time at my surgery, and I appreciated the helpfulness of the staff. But the receptionist was unamused. My blood results were back. To my surprise, they diagnosed me with Lyme disease, a bacterial infection transmitted by ticks. It turned out that slippery little fecker was responsible for all my symptoms. The doctor assured me the symptoms would pass and asked me to take another blood test. Although relieved menopause wasn't the culprit—that was one mountain I was not yet ready to climb—I knew I still had a challenging journey ahead.

Chapter Twenty-Four

A Fish out Of Water

Inspired by the learning session with author Helen, I delved deeper into writing. I saw an advert on social media for a monthly poetry club at a nearby arts centre. Attendance was free, so I downloaded a ticket. I wasn't entirely sure it was me, even though I'd loved poetry as a kid. But it must be a bit me, otherwise I wouldn't have read the advert or got a ticket. And I'd never know until I tried. I made my way there, feeling more than a little nervous. I was never usually nervous about meeting new people. What was wrong with me? Was it the booze that had made me confident? I loosened the buttons of my coat to cool down and took a few deep breaths. Come on, Lisa! I told myself. It's just a few ladies who liked to play with words, for heaven's sake! Then it hit me why I was feeling so anxious. I would have to fess up to being an alcoholic and in recovery. (How long would I need to say, 'in recovery'? Would it be forever?)

I could not avoid the issue. My poems were all about alcohol addiction, and detox in particular. I'd never spoken out loud to strangers about what I was going through. But I no longer felt embarrassed. I was proud of my journey and everything I'd achieved. Alcoholism was a taboo topic, so often brushed under the carpet. People sometimes didn't quite know what to say to me, so they swiftly changed the subject and moved on. Why is it socially unacceptable to talk about people becoming addicted to something that's so highly addictive? Yet someone talking about the struggle to quit smoking twenty cigarettes is considered perfectly normal.

Me and my two new classmates smiled at each other and sat down before the course leader introduced herself and set the scene for what was going to happen.

'Reading our most intimate thoughts out loud in our poetry can make us feel vulnerable,' she said, reassuring us that nobody would be judging. Tears welled up in my eyes and my chest tightened. But I was determined to be heard. Raising my hand, I blurted everything out.

'I'm feeling really vulnerable right now,' I said. 'You see, my poems are about being addicted to alcohol. I used to drink a bit. A lot. I was an alcoholic.'

And then I burst into tears.

'I'm sorry,' I said. 'I've never said that out loud to strangers. I feel better now it's out in the open—but I also feel like an unstable idiot!'

The three of them stared back at me in silence. I sensed their shock. Finally, one woman thanked me for 'sharing'. I hated that phrase. What was I even doing there?

The tutor invited us to tell everyone a little about ourselves and the woman on my right introduced herself as 'Goat'. Now I really felt like a square in a room full of circles, a fish out of water. The others weren't like me. They were good people, earthy and wholesome. How was I going to get out of this? Why did I get myself into such tricky situations? The first poem to be read was on a piece of A4 paper. I couldn't take in what she was saying over the clanging panic that mine was only four sentences, more like a naughty greetings card full of swearing than the flowery words she was pouring out. She said words I didn't even know, and I jotted a few down to Google later. I could have kicked myself for coming. The common idiot had come to show the educated, well-rounded people how stupid she was. Why did I always feel I wasn't quite good enough? I didn't even know them!

And then came my turn. I was terrified about the scathing critiques that awaited me. And then I remembered that only minutes earlier I'd burst into tears—no way in hell would they diss my poem in case I had another meltdown! They had no choice but to listen intently. My ordeal was all over in a matter of seconds. One lady asked to have another look at it. The other said it was 'raw and full of emotion'. It turned out I'd written a ballad poem. I didn't know what that meant, but they seemed to like it. Although I relaxed towards the end of the session, I decided not to go back. I already had enough pressure in my life. Besides, I needed to focus my attention on the book I was trying to write. I would shelve the poetry club for another time.

That night I was meeting some old work colleagues I hadn't seen for eighteen months, and I raced home to get ready. The gang of us used to go out drinking together, so this was yet another test and I was feeling the itch. I drove there and soon people were asking why I was on soft drinks. This time, they got a straight answer.

'I don't drink any more,' I said.

I could see their shock. 'Don't you miss it?' someone asked. Of course I fucking missed it! But I started asking myself how much I missed it. Soon I was chair-dancing to some old northern soul music. I could just have one pint of cider, have a little dance and then drive home. But I quickly remembered the reason I didn't drink. I looked up to see a woman at our table stuffing her face with a paper plate piled high with food from the buffet. Pissed, her eyes half closed and eating with her mouth wide open. She had egg mayonnaise all over her face and breadcrumbs down her top. Nope. Another Diet Coke for me, squire. Whenever I felt the itch, I seemed to get some sort of sign, little reminders of why I had made the right choice. Someone out there was watching over me and helping me whenever I came up against an obstacle. I was once told by a medium that

I had a spirit guide, an Indian guy called Meynell. Maybe it was him. I drove home stone cold sober and enjoyed a cup of tea in bed. All right, I might not have been Party Lisa any more—here I was in bed before ten o'clock on a Saturday night—but I still had as much fun as the others. And in the morning, I would be bright-eyed and bushy-tailed to do whatever I choose.

Chapter Twenty-Five

Dropping a Clanger

I became bored at work, even though I hadn't been in my new job for long. With my new-found energy and positivity, my days were dragging and I no longer felt satisfaction from my endless list of mundane tasks. My focus was now on personal growth, and where I was, I had no room to grow. When someone mentioned a job going at Recovery Connections during our group session, it sounded right up my street—but it would mean the end of my support. If I worked for them, I wouldn't be able to attend meetings any more. The thought made my blood run cold. I was nowhere near ready. I knew I needed continuing support, so I decided not to apply. Meanwhile, I kept getting braver. I even told the lady at Specsavers I was a recovering alcoholic. She had asked what plans I had for the rest of the day and I told her I was meeting my partner and the dog in the pub.

NO DRINK FOR ME

'Ooh, a couple of cheeky wines to finish the weekend off,' she said.

'No, I don't drink.'

She asked me why. Like kids sharing secrets I leaned further into the cubicle and she leaned in to meet me.

'I used to be an alcoholic,' I whispered.

'I think my boyfriend is,' she replied, equally quietly.

I burst out laughing.

'Why do we feel the need to whisper? Are we embarrassed that someone will hear?'

After all, if we were discussing stopping smoking, we wouldn't whisper. She agreed. I sat back in my chair, and we chatted for a while. I told her how long it had been since my last drink and how I believed I'd finally succeeded this time. I recommended our local support group and gave her the details. That conversation made me realise just how many people are affected by alcoholism. I hoped that by opening up to me she would get her boyfriend the help he needs. By now I often preached about the importance of not being embarrassed. You should be proud that you're dealing with your addiction. But I knew I was also the biggest hypocrite because my alcohol-free Instagram page was still anonymous and I never posted a picture of myself. Practise what you preach, Lisa!

I'd heard about the Change Grow Live graduation day. Each client who had completed the CBT programme wore a cap and gown, received a certificate and attended a ceremony where they rang a bell. I loved the idea and was looking forward to mine—until the time came. I woke up in the morning not sure how I felt about it any more...

A. I would feel like a plonker in a purple cap and gown. Purple isn't my colour.

B. I didn't have a degree, so I would feel like a fraud.

C. Was ringing a bell necessary? It all seemed a little over the top.

As I got ready, I considered not going. I could have my own little graduation ceremony instead, going out for the day and treating myself to lunch and some fancy clothes or jewellery. I used to love going on treat trips by myself, browsing the shops and then heading to a pub for lunch. But I would always meet some randoms and end up on a bender with my new best friends. Perhaps going to graduation would be a safer option, I decided. My logic went like this...

A. I would look all wizardy in the purple gown and I rather suit hats, especially hats with tassels.

B. Degree or not, I'd worked bloody hard to wear that outfit. I feel like Satan himself has shat on me so many times.

C. If there was a bell, then I was ringing it. In fact, I deserved to fly-kick that bell along Stockton High Street with a crowd of thousands cheering me on.

I turned up at the centre, armed with a Diet Coke. There were about eight people there, but I only recognised a couple of the staff and I immediately felt awkward. I sat between a couple of ladies and tried to join in with their conversation. Another woman joined us and asked what I was in for. I laughed. It sounded as though we were in prison! Her cheeks flushed bright pink and I was ashamed for laughing.

'I'm in for alcohol,' I said.

She was new and had a long list of questions that she rattled out as soon as I'd answered the previous one. How long had I been off the drink? Was it hard? Is it forever? How do I cope? What about holidays?

'Stopping was the best thing I've ever done,' I said. 'I only wish I'd done it years ago.'

Then I told her I had a secret and leaned in to whisper.

'When you're drinking, you're not really living,' I told her. 'You're just existing with a hangover. There's a better way to live.'

She sat back and looked lost in her thoughts for a few moments before she responded.

'You're right,' she said. 'My life is one big hangover.'

We talked about our drinking habits and giggled about the excuses she used, both to herself and everyone else in her life. I'd used most of them myself.

'It's taken me until now to realise they are just that,' she said. 'Excuses.'

I told her she was already on the right path. The hardest move is admitting to yourself that you're an alcoholic and then seeking help. It takes guts to ask for help. But my new friend told me she felt like a fraud for coming to the graduation ceremony and said she shouldn't be wearing the gown.

'Why do you think that?' I asked.

'Because I was rat-arsed last night,' she confessed and we both burst out laughing again.

Before I could respond we were being welcomed for the ceremony. I couldn't stop laughing at how silly I looked in my cap and gown. Looking around, I could see everyone else felt just as embarrassed. But when my name was called, I walked down the metal steps to accept my certificate, then trotted over to the bell and gave it a loud ring. So what if I look ridiculous? I thought, as I clanged for all I was worth. I'm proud of what I've achieved. And then the clanger came off in my hand. I know they say pride comes before a fall, but it's not usually that quick! Once again, I was the subject of everyone's amusement. Why did it always happen to me? I felt like a female Norman Wisdom. To make matters worse, someone had captured my hilarious moment on camera.

My over-enthusiastic bell-ringing technique was the major topic of conversation as we enjoyed the buffet after the ceremony. Then I recognised a girl from the Thursday night group. She told me she was twenty-nine, so calling her young was a clear signal I was getting on a bit. Her name was Charlie and this was her second go at recovery. She had been alcohol-free for one year and four days and thought she was 'cured', so she tried to introduce alcohol back into her life. Before long she was back to drinking daily. Once an alcoholic, as they say, always an alcoholic. We lost ourselves in conversation about the difficulties we'd faced and the challenges life had thrown our way. She asked for my phone number, and I added her to our

WhatsApp group. I realised in that moment I had been destined to meet Charlie. I was convinced our paths were meant to cross. I wasn't sure whether I needed her or she needed me, but I knew she would be in my life.

I felt raw and emotional as I drove home that evening. But I was also proud. I had just cleared another hurdle on my recovery journey. So why was I still ashamed to 'come out' on Instagram? The time had come to practise what I preached. I chose a couple of snaps from the ceremony, including a selfie of me wearing my mortarboard hat.

'I used to be embarrassed about being in recovery, but how proud of myself I have become,' I wrote. I paused for a moment and then sent it out into the virtual universe. I suddenly experienced an overwhelming feeling of relief. I was freer somehow, released from my cage of humiliation. I wanted to smash every stereotype that was out there and take away the stigma of being an alcoholic. More people should talk about it. I invented a new first rule of sober club—never stop talking about sober club! Once I started, there was no stopping me. I know I talked about it too much, especially at work. You have to think about staying sober every day to stay focused. It's like being on a diet plan. You need to really focus on every meal and sometimes join a class to share your journey with others. Sobriety was the best thing that had ever happened to me, and I wanted to tell the world. Everyone else who was suffering needed to know there can be a happy ending. There is life after alcohol. For the first few months I couldn't envisage my life without drink in it.

A wedding without champagne, Christmas without sherry, a funeral without whisky or a christening without prosecco had seemed impossible. Now I could look to a future that didn't involve alcohol. I would still be at the weddings, christenings, funerals and celebrating Christmas, but now I would be present and enjoy the moment. I don't think I had ever been truly present; I was always in my foggy 'Lisa land'. Now I could soak up the atmosphere and appreciate the time I spent with family and friends. I spoke freely about my sobriety now, without the shadow of shame. I felt more open talking to my family, too. Jimi shared my story with some of his friends and said they were all pleased for me. I loved him being so open. I'd expected him to shy away from the topic and certainly didn't think he would confide in his friends. If I'm honest, I thought he might feel embarrassed about me. It's not usually a subject young lads and their mates talk about. He told me some had spoken about their own issues with smoking weed and how they wanted to stop or have more control. I was so pleased he felt he could talk to me about these important subjects. I wanted him to be able to tell me anything. My parents were becoming more open to talking about addiction as well. They could see how much happier I was and told me how well I'd done. Danny's support remained constant. He regularly reminded me how proud he was of me. I don't think either of us could quite believe how well I had done.

Chapter Twenty-Six

Charlie's Angel

We settled into our new home nicely. I had rescued a bench that was about to be thrown into a skip. Although tatty and worn around the edges, I could see it still had lots of life in it. Now, if ever you hear anybody talking about sanding a bench, do them a favour and tell them not to. A couple of hours of sanding and a quick lick of stain would bring it right back, I thought. But when I reached my third weekend in a row of sanding, my back and hands were killing me and I could taste the dust in my mouth. I had started out rubbing the surface by hand, but halfway through the task a trusty DIY pal offered me his electric sander. I was grateful for his kindness at first, but in no time I could have cheerfully strangled him. The new sander worked a treat and took a lot of the hard work out of the job. Unfortunately, the second half looked better than the first, so I had to go over the first part again with the new tool. Just what I needed. Danny helpfully named it the eternal bench. The work was backbreaking and frustrating, but

I also had a lot of time to myself, and it got me thinking. I was just like this bench. Tattered and worn, but little by little I was shedding layer after layer of old varnish and finding the real Lisa underneath. Much like the sanding, I was getting into the cracks and corners of my life, restoring the beauty of my own grain. I could so easily have been tossed into a skip and left on the scrapheap, but now I knew I was worth all the hard work. By the time I'd finished sanding, I'd made friends with the bench again. I even apologised for all the swear words I'd called it. When I had finished, it was going to be my thinking bench. I would drink cups of tea and collect my thoughts while sitting there. I couldn't wait. I applied two coats of wood stain and made some cushions to finish it off. It looked amazing and I was delighted with myself. I shared the before and after photos with all my friends, who couldn't believe the dramatic transformation. All my hard work had paid off.

Charlie and I shared a few WhatsApp messages and arranged to venture out together. Our sister recovery group in nearby Middlesbrough held an alcohol-free social meet up once a fortnight. We wanted to give them our support, as well as being an opportunity to meet other people who understood us. This week had a slightly different agenda, being a film festival. Recovery groups from across the UK had entered a competition to make a short video.

We arrived at the venue and everyone made us feel welcome. The big screen was up and they had laid out popcorn on the table, with free tea and coffee available. Charlie also ordered nachos and hotdogs. That was my diet chucked out of the window.

I recognised a few faces from our Facebook group and Charlie saw some girls she knew from Alcoholics Anonymous. The compere explained that the videos all shared the same theme—'I am'—which made me think of my mantra, *'I am Lisa Peacock'*. The films examined different views of recovery and the various stages we go through, he said. He warned they could be upsetting and might even be a trigger for some of us. As soon as the first clip started, I felt a lump in my throat. For a moment I was outside of myself, looking in. How the hell did I get here? Where did my life go so wrong? But as quickly as these thoughts arrived, positivity swept them away. *You've come so far! You've actually done it. You're in recovery. You're not just coping and managing, you're thriving!* I was enjoying life and knew precisely where I was. I was finally finding the real me—and you know what? I liked her!

The films blew me away. A child's view of her alcoholic mother. A brother wishing his sister would stop drinking and take care of her kids. A retired businessman so lonely he turned to booze. A young priest struggling to cope with challenges in his own life and the traumas of the people he served. Young men and women drinking to mask their lack of self-confidence. I just wanted to give each of them a big hug and tell them everything was all right. And I was one of these people. I deserved a cuddle. Charlie beside me deserved a hug too, and I felt tempted to offer her one, but I hardly know her. She might think I'm weird.

I looked around the room at all the unique personalities and the ages of these people. This was my recovery family. I wanted to get involved with them and show my support. By the looks of Facebook, they even had a community garden. I've always wanted to grow something. When the evening ended, the compere thanked us both for coming and I dropped Charlie home. The night was wonderful.

I lay awake in bed for hours thinking of my life in a movie. What would I put in a three-minute film? Would I play myself or ask someone else? What would the world think of my story? It would start with a night out with friends...

We're all dressed up, bouncy hair and manicured nails. The disco ball turning. We sip exotic cocktails and champagne from ice buckets. We're having so much fun, laughing and posing for photographs that make perfect Facebook posts. Just girls having fun in full colour. When the night ends, I'm in the taxi alone, and the film turns black and white. The focus blurs as I make my way into the twenty-four-hour garage for two more bottles of wine. The film ends with me slumped on the sofa drinking alone in my party dress, my night only just beginning...

I sometimes think my story isn't as dramatic or poignant as other people's. Listening to some of them, the volume of my drinking was far lower. I heard stories of litres of vodka, whisky or rum and four bottles of wine a day. I managed to stick to two bottles a night during the week, although there were no limits at the weekend. I had a job and had to drive to work every morning. But towards the end of my drinking, I didn't feel like working any more. I wanted to slip into morning and daytime drinking. My hangovers were getting worse and my alcoholic remorse was consuming me. I knew I was on the verge of losing everything. But alcoholism isn't about how much you drink or what time of the day. It's about the thoughts racing through your head. The constant thinking about booze. Should I or shouldn't I? My conscience saying no and my inner devil jumping up and down on my shoulder carrying two shot glasses and saying, 'Let's go!' Drinking wasn't just taking over my brain, it was taking over my body too. I looked terrible. Obese, sluggish, tired. My hair was greasy and my skin was becoming red and shiny. I looked like exactly what I was—a drunk. I was obsessed with drinking. But now I had taken the chance to step back and analyse my life after being preoccupied with alcohol from the age of thirteen. People often asked how I became an alcoholic. Are we born alcoholics? I don't think I was. I had a variety of reasons. Where I lived, in a working-class area of Teesside where heavy drinking was commonplace. Everyone seemed to finish their working day in one of the many social clubs dotted around the estates. There was the lack of rules at home when I was growing up. I could do what I wanted. I'm not in any way blaming my parents, or anyone else for that matter. I'm just looking at the factors that made me different. I hung around with much older kids who were doing more grown-up stuff than kids my age. I aspired to be like them. Peer pressure, I suppose you'd call it. Then there was my all-or-nothing attitude. I always had to push boundaries and go to the extremes. I craved danger and excitement. I learned addiction from such a young age that I knew no different.

After enjoying the film night so much, I decided to join a Recovery Games trip. People gather from all over the country and compete as teams to win a trophy, and Recovery Connections had organised a coach. The idea was to celebrate our success and break down the stigmas surrounding addiction. I took my seat on the coach with about forty other people, from Sunderland, Washington, Stockton and Middlesbrough. I couldn't help looking around and wondering what each person's story was. I would have loved to delve into their lives and see what had happened. It would make a fascinating TV documentary that would open people's eyes and stop them being so judgemental.

The event itself was amazing and the camaraderie between participants was something else. Our team, the Stockton Spartans, competed in Gladiators-style challenges such as duelling, the wrecking ball, the leap of faith and Thor's hammer. My moment of glory came in the aqua assault course. I had to wear a wetsuit, and I didn't have a wetsuit body. One of us had to swim to the pontoon, scramble across the assault course and return to tag the other, who then did the same. My teammate went first, and I had too much thinking time while I waited for her return. My tight wetsuit restricted my chest, and I had a buoyancy aid fastened snugly against my body. It made me feel a bit panicky, and I told the lifeguard I needed to get my suit off. The opposition team heard me. But did they secretly think, *Yes, we'll get an extra point here, we'll win easily*? No. They rallied round to support me, surrounding me with words of kindness and encouragement.

'Come on, you can do it! Challenge yourself—we'll cheer you on!'

I was both shocked and moved.

'You're right,' I said. 'If I can get through recovery, I can get through this!'

Once I set off, I loved it—and when I completed my swim back, the crowd erupted. Being around others who had been through what I had and making these connections with other people in recovery was just what I needed. It's what works. Nobody took sides. We all stood together as one.

Later in the day I heard a Mancunian guy being interviewed and he said something so true.

'We are living proof that you don't need drugs or alcohol to have a good time.'

Bang on, my friend. I applaud you.

The festival was almost a magical wonderland, a recovery bubble with no judgement, all standing together as one. The excitement and sheer joy I experienced that day only increased my new-found desire to be involved in recovery and help other people. Imagine having that much fun and actually being at work! What could be better than being paid to be involved in other people's recovery? Helping someone in their darkest and most vulnerable hour would be like a gift to me—I've been in that dark place, and it's gruesome. I was ready now.

***

Danny had made plans to join a friend to walk a stretch of the Camino de Santiago in Spain. We had never spent more than two days apart in almost ten years, and I knew I would miss him terribly. As we hugged goodbye, he reminded me how much he loved me. He promised to call and take lots of photos, and then I waved him off as he headed to the airport. I was so pleased he was going on a little adventure. He worked hard and deserved a break. But the second the latch dropped on the garden gate, I started thinking about the bottle of Jameson's whiskey I knew was in the cupboard under the kitchen sink. I could drink it right now and nobody else in the world would know. It could be my little secret. I thought about what people often said to me. 'You've done so well. You can just have the one and control it now.' In my dreams! I was terrified that just one sip of alcohol would undo all the work I had done and would rapidly spiral out of control. Was it worth it? Absolutely not! I hadn't gone through all those awful nights feeling suicidal to go back to my old habits. I'd walked barefoot through fields of broken glass with flame throwers firing from both sides to get where I was. I'd been through hell, and nobody even noticed. I'd squared up toe-to-toe with Satan himself and spat at him, 'Bring it on—do your worst! If only people could see the scars inside, they would know how I held myself together with glue and gaffer tape. But my disease was almost invisible.

Charlie was celebrating her birthday the weekend Danny was away. She was turning thirty, so it was a big one. Even though we had just met, I wanted to get her a little something. I had a little nosy around the shops and found a small pin badge of a guardian angel to keep her safe. I also bought a wish bracelet. You tie it on and make a wish, and when the bracelet falls off, your wish comes true. Or so the label said. I just needed a birthday card, but I couldn't find a single one that didn't feature alcohol. It's not that I thought pictures of drink would be a trigger for Charlie, but I had never noticed this before. It only reinforced my theory that we're all being programmed to drink, with subliminal messages all around us. By the time I had rejected cards showing champagne flutes, cocktail glasses and bottles of gin and prosecco, I was hell bent on finding a drink-free card. In the end I had to settle for a child's card with a panda on the front. The girl on the checkout was glad when I left. I'd only had a teeny-weeny rant though.

Not long after Danny came home we arranged to go to a VW festival for the weekend. Now, we don't actually have a VW, we have a Land Rover, but hey, who's checking? We sang together all the way, laughing until we cried. I'm not sure if I dare write this—I'll definitely lose my Rock Chick badge—but we put S Club 7 on. We both blasted out *Reach for the Stars* at the top of our voices, me using a can of hairspray for a mic. I loved it when we were both in a silly mood.

Everyone was already drinking by the time we arrived at the camp, and some were already drunk. But they were all very welcoming. Someone even offered me a can of Fosters lager, which I politely declined. Our friends soon joined us and we headed for the bar. I'd smuggled my alcohol-free red wine in. I watched the band set up. What sounded like an AC/DC reference in their name, Back 2 Black, made me hopeful it would be my kind of music. The thunder of the kick drum during the sound check made my heart skip a beat. I love most live music, but the band weren't exactly what I was expecting. They took their name from the Amy Winehouse song, not the similarly titled AC/DC album, *Back in Black*. Still, the singer had an incredible voice and they pulled a few hits out of the bag—Stevie Wonder, The Police and Bruce Springsteen favourites. And then they played the introductory bars of *Valerie*. Every time I hear that song it reminds me of being kicked out of a hotel bar. A few friends and I had been to watch the Foo Fighters and we were all fired up and having a few wines and shots in the hotel bar. When Valerie came on we all broke out singing at the top of our voices and the manager politely asked us to leave.

'I'm going nowhere until I've finished my drink,' I slurred. That's when two gorilla-sized doormen escorted me out.

This time, though, I didn't have alcohol to help me shed my inhibitions. It might sound silly, but I'd never danced sober in my whole adult life. Tonight, though, I'd promised myself I would dance. Maybe the key was pretending I was drunk! Drinking alcohol-free red wine, nobody else would know if I was drunk or not. As the dance floor filled up with screaming ladies, I knew my moment had arrived. I didn't quite make it to the floor, but I had a little bop where we stood. I grinned like a Cheshire cat and my body loosened up as I jigged about, clapping my hands. A tidal wave of joy overwhelmed me. At that moment, I was free. I was sober, and I was having fun. My eyes filled with happy tears, and I looked up to see Danny watching me. He knew how much this meant to me, and he could see how happy I was. Placing his powerful arms around my waist, he swayed with me in time with the music and whispered in my ear.

'I love the way you dance.'

When I was drinking I would have laughed, but in the clarity of sobriety I closed my eyes and inhaled his warmth and his goodness. I hadn't made it through the last few months with my strength alone. Danny had been by my side the entire time. I rubbed my cheek against his and felt thankful for everything I had in my life.

Chapter Twenty-Seven

The Final Countdown

Less than two weeks to go until my one-year anniversary. I'd been sober for 352 days. How the heck did we get here? I will admit I was as scared as I had ever been in my life. What would one year feel like? Would I have the urge to drink? Would I feel like I was just starting out on day one? I used to count the days and look forward to my year being up so I could have a drink, but now that thought filled me with dread. I never wanted to go there again. I didn't want to sit in a trendy bar with a glass of crisp white wine because I knew I would want a second crisp white wine, followed by a third and so on. The thought of having such cravings and 'needing' in my life terrified me. That demoralising cycle of wanting, craving, drinking, the hangovers, the guilt, the shame. Looking back, I can see how damaged I was. Alcohol was my driving force. My reason for getting up and going to work. Whatever I was doing, whoever I was with, I counted down the hours until I could have the drink I 'deserved'. I was banging my head against a brick wall, day in, day out, hoping it would stop, but doing nothing about it. I never thought I had the courage or the determination to change my entire life. It had been no walk in the park. I almost buckled many times and it would have been so easy to pick up a drink. But I didn't. And I didn't want to go back to being that person. I had a new life now. I was focused, motivated and positive. Finally in the driving seat. I was healthy and well and had lost several stones in weight, gained self-confidence and, more importantly, earned a new respect for myself. The good person I always knew I had inside me was now present every day. My relationships had grown and I respected people more. I appreciated my life now and realised I was one lucky woman to have everyone and everything I had. And I was going to hold it all tight to my heart.

Danny, Jimi and I planned to spend my one-year soberversary in Pisa visiting Rocchina, Danny's last surviving aunt in Italy. Aunty Rock was a strong, motivated lady with the heart of a lion. She welcomed me and my son into her family with open arms when we first met her in 2014 and she is special to all of us. Sadly, Danny had lost his grandma, Maria, in 2019, and Aunty Rock was the closest thing we had to her. She grew her own vegetables and taught me about the land, and we spent hours chatting and reminiscing about her life. She had come to England and trained to be a nurse at Scarborough Hospital. There she learned to love The Beatles, the lady with the big teeth (Cilla Black) and the lady with the black eyes (Dusty Springfield). She was building a new life for herself in England until her mother passed away and she had to return to Italy to care for her father. She told me about working as a machinist in some of the top Milan fashion houses and meeting her husband, Michael, who had passed away. She had worked hard throughout her life and at eighty-four, showed no signs of slowing down.

I couldn't let such an important milestone in my life pass without marking it. I decided to carry out a little photo shoot. I ordered a huge foil Number One and made a cardboard sign saying, 'One year'. It was out of character, but this was something that I needed to celebrate. Never in my wildest dreams did I ever think I would get here. I ordered two new dresses and began the drama of what I was going to wear. I'd always hated photographs of myself. When I told Jimi what I was planning, I expected rolling eyes and a 'Do we have to?' But he surprised and delighted me when he said it was a great idea. I was struck by how my stopping drinking had affected him. He had shown nothing but support and has told me how proud he is more than anyone else. Opening up my vulnerable side to him was hard. I was supposed to be the strong one. But doing so had taught him some valuable lessons. He now better understood the importance of staying in control of alcohol. He was patient, understanding and didn't judge. And this entire journey had brought us closer together. He now knew I trusted him and valued his opinion. I didn't want to visit Italy for this special day without him.

I told him about the trip when we went swimming together one day. It was such a normal, simple thing to do, but I thoroughly enjoyed the experience. It took me back to when Jimi was little. After our swim we were always starving and with our hair still damp, we'd go for chips doused with salt and vinegar, and then sit on a bench, swinging our legs as we wolfed them down. I could still see Jimi scrunching his face up because I'd put too much vinegar on. Now, we did it all again, laughing and joking and watching the world go by. But I felt pangs of sadness and guilt as I realised I wouldn't have done this before I had stopped drinking. I would either have been in the pub or too hungover. I felt tempted to ask Jimi how he felt when I was drinking. Did he realise I had a problem? Did he feel let down or left out? But I clammed up, afraid to ask because I thought I knew the answer, and I didn't want to spoil our afternoon. I did my best as a mum, but I knew I could have done better. I lost myself to addiction during Jimi's teenage years. I tried not to dwell on the past any more, but sometimes it crept up on me. But what counted was what happened now.

Only now I was alcohol free did I realise how obsessed I was. Brainwashed. Drink was everywhere. All my peers drank, TV adverts told me drinking was cool, we drank to mark every celebration, happy or sad. I remembered being told not to take drugs at school and warned of the dangers, but I don't recall being warned about alcohol. And yet it's one of the most addictive drugs on the planet. Things have changed over the years and we do have warning signs on alcohol, information about units and restrictions on drink deals in bars. But Wetherspoons is still allowed to open and serve alcohol at eight o'clock in the morning. Society still glamorises drinking. We still see signs saying, 'It's gin o'clock!' 'Nobody gets out sober' and 'Stay calm and drink wine'. We've even made gin pink. David Beckham makes Hague Club look cool and Jean-Claude van Damme shows us how drinking Coors has kept him flexible.

Even in these later months of recovery, I still thought about having a drink. I still told myself that maybe I had been cured now. Friends often told me, 'But you're OK now Lisa, you're not addicted any more.' Now this may sound strong, and I'm not understating the horrors of the disease, but I liken being an alcoholic to having had cancer. If you have had it, you will always have it. It will always be in the back of your mind. You will willingly attend scans to check up on it. Similarly, I will always be aware I was an alcoholic. A beast lives inside me and I have to stay well and focused to stop it from coming out on top again. I will always keep my eye on it and attend meetings to keep it at bay.

It's hard to explain to someone that it only takes one drink. Why were people so keen for me to join them? They were obsessed! There is a saying in AA, one is too many, but 100 is not enough. It's like telling an ex-smoker to only have a cigarette on Thursdays. Addictions don't work like that; they aren't so benevolent. One can of cider opens the door to two, then three, then four, and before you know it you're in a corridor lined with shiny new doors to open. I have opened those doors before. I know exactly what lies behind them all, and I deserve better. I'm keeping them tightly closed, double-bolted and padlocked. I want the door bricked up, plastered and wallpapered over, and then disguised as a normal wall. One drink to me would be the kiss of death. No thank you.

Chapter Twenty-Eight

How the Saints Stole My Soberversary

My GP prescribed more antibiotics for my Lyme disease because the first course wasn't strong enough. I had to take them for three whole weeks. I felt the familiar pang in my stomach that I always did when someone mentioned antibiotics. I panicked in case I was told I couldn't drink with them. I don't think I had ever completed a full course. I needn't worry this time. I sometimes forgot I didn't drink any more.

'You won't be able to have a one-year celebratory glass of wine in Italy now,' Danny said when I came home. I make a mental note to update him on the fact I don't want one.

As usual, my knees were knocking and my chest was tight and I was breathless with anxiety as we made our way to Manchester Airport. At forty-four years old I was still terrified of flying. It will never leave me. I just find different ways to cope with it.

We passed through security and I was disappointed that the bar didn't offer any alcohol-free drinks. Instead, I opted for a cup of tea. I'd turned into a bit of a tea bag. Danny ordered a lager and Jimi wanted a cider. When the waitress delivered the drinks to our table, I took a quick sniff of the cider. It smelled like heaven and took me back to so many places—some amazing, some disastrous. I blushed as I remembered how some of our previous holidays had turned out. On a seven-night trip to Morocco, I fell asleep drunk on the flight and woke up in Marrakech Airport. That was a perfect flight for me. As soon as I reached the resort I started drinking again and that was it—I spent the full week in a groggy haze. By the end of the holiday the bar staff were calling me Rosé Lisa. The glasses were so small I would order two wines at a time. It was all-inclusive, after all. This holiday was going to be worlds apart from that one. I would remember everything and not suffer from hangover anxiety ('beer fear', I called it). I wouldn't manipulate every day around drinking, 'accidentally' landing in bars whenever my levels were low. I planned to exercise each morning and savour every minute of our time there, enjoying the last sunshine I would see for a few months as we headed into a dreary North-East winter. For the first time in my life we had a full row of empty seats, so I curled up with my music playing through my headphones, and before I knew it, the captain announced we were descending.

We were greeted by warm sunshine as we climbed down the steps. It had been three years since we had seen our Italian relatives and they were there with open arms to greet us at Galileo Airport arrivals. Back at the house, Aunty Rock had prepared a feast. It was her birthday and she had bought some wine for me. She wasn't drinking, but she wanted me to. She looked deflated when I told her I didn't drink any more.

'I bought it especially for you,' she said.

I shoved a slice of garlic bread into my mouth and ignored her pleas. Instead, I told her about our plan to visit Pisa on November 1st. Aunty Rock soon dashed that idea. The centre of the city would be closed for the Festa Di Tutti i Santi (All Saints' Day), she explained. All Saints Day was a bank holiday in Italy, a time when people visited family and friends to celebrate. I was livid. The saints had stolen my soberversary! I'd bought a balloon and even made a bloody sign—if anything, it should be St Lisa's Day! And then I realised how selfish I was to expect the whole of Italy to abandon their traditions just because I'd stopped boozing. It wouldn't hurt me to celebrate differently. I would just tinker with my plans. Aunty Rock wasn't giving up her plan to pour wine down my throat, though.

'It's the best wine you can buy in Italy,' she said. 'Why not try it?'

I wanted to scream at the top of my lungs, 'Because I don't fucking drink, stop pestering me!'

Instead, I clammed up. How could I explain that I was an alcoholic? Panicking, I looked around for help. Danny and Jimi had noticed my tense body language and rabbit-in-the-headlight eyes and immediately intervened, asking if they could try some. I offered to open the bottle, taking the opportunity for a break from the clamouring intensity of an Italian family meal. I took the wine to the kitchen and pulled the cork out. A quick sniff told me this was a 3.99-euro bottle at best. I wouldn't brush my teeth with that! I'll pass, thank you. But I knew it was going to be a long week if I had to dodge the bottle every day.

We spent the next day lounging in the sun and wandering around a local market. Afterwards, we walked to the marina and settled outside a café to watch the sunset, Danny with a beer and Jimi with a glass of wine. I felt an urge to scratch the itch and have just a tiny glass of wine. After all, sunsets and wine had always gone together. My favourite holiday treat. Would these cravings ever leave me? They were weaker now, though. Just a tiny flame, flickering now and then, rather than the out-of-control inferno of those first few weeks of sobriety twelve months ago.

I pondered all of this as the sun dipped and touched the ocean. I can take it or leave it now, I told myself. And then I remembered a conversation the first time I met Charlie. She didn't drink for a year and four days. She thought she was cured and could drink in a controlled way. Within a month she was back to her old drinking habits. Was it really worth the risk for me? No. A drink would give me one quick buzz, but I would want another one. The guilt would be back. I would have thrown away the last twelve months and let myself and my peers down. And I would definitely need a wee on the way home!

We visited Pisa a day earlier than planned. Of course, we headed for the Leaning Tower, which would be such an iconic backdrop for a photo. We struggled to find the right position, snaking through the crowds trying to get the perfect shot of them pushing the tower over. When we found our spot, I pulled the cardboard sign from my bag. Together with my usual reluctance to have my photo taken, the sign made me even more self-conscious. It didn't help that a stunning model-type girl was alongside me, pulling some spectacular poses. Probably an influencer, whatever they are. Beside her I felt big and frumpy. Passing tourists were more interested in me and my sign, though, and I noticed Jimi laughing at me and my embarrassment. So I took a deep breath and remembered why I was here. None of them knew how hard I had worked for this moment. It had been a twelve-month war, with me on the frontline every day, mustering every ounce of inner strength I had. I had the battle scars to prove it. I deserved to be here with my sign, and the other tourists should part like the Red Sea, leaving only me in the shot. Get out of my way and start that camera rolling!

We spent the rest of the day strolling around shops, eating pizza and ice cream. The winter sun caressed us and I could indulge in one of my favourite pastimes, people-watching. I realised I no longer wondered what their favourite drinks were any more. I just watched them go by on their merry way.

Chapter Twenty-Nine

The Eagle has Landed

I opened my eyes. My big day was here at last. I had done it! I checked my banking app—I had saved a whopping £3,650. A rush of happiness and pride overwhelmed me. Little old me! I had set out to do something and I achieved it. Today was going to be a special day. Yes, the saints had upstaged me, but I was over that now. Almost, anyway. Danny brought me a cup of tea.

'Happy one year,' he said, but he didn't seem too enthusiastic. I thought he would have been a little more excited for me.

I woke Jimi, and as soon as he opened his eyes he congratulated me.

'Happy one year, Mam. I'm so proud of you.'

It was a poignant moment. I could see how much he meant it as he beamed at me.

A delicious breakfast spread awaited us in the dining room. Croissants, jams, marmalades, cheeses, meats, juice and fruit. Danny and Jimi were both grinning. The tinkers had planned this! I was smiling and wiping tears away. I felt loved and appreciated. At the centre of the buffet was a small velvet box and Danny told me to open it. Inside was a stunning pendant, a silver eagle decorated with mother-of-pearl, jet and turquoise. A wise woman once told me I was an eagle among hens and I just needed to learn to fly, and so I did. I had spread my wings out wide and I was soaring. Such a thoughtful gift. I put the necklace on and held it close. I sometimes took my partner and family for granted, as we all do. When I was drinking, Danny would drape his arm over me as we lay together in bed. I thought nothing of it back then. Now I could feel its warmth and appreciated him protecting and keeping me safe. And I could feel the love. Such a basic gesture, but it meant everything to me. I was determined never to forget the support Danny had given me. He had held my hand the entire way, steadied me when I was shaking and comforted me at my lowest point. He pulled me up from my despair and encouraged me to push myself forward. But most important of all, he had always believed in me. He knew I could do it and he told me so. He was my soulmate and my best friend. I vowed at that moment never to take my family for granted again. I was going to appreciate them more and make sure we spent quality time together. I owed these two men everything. They were my reasons for getting well.

Charlie had sent me to Italy with a parcel, only to be opened today. As I unwrapped the paper, the contents sparkled in the sun. It was a 'one-year sober' chip from Alcoholics Anonymous. I didn't go to AA, but she knew I liked the tokens. I stepped outside into the early morning sunshine to get some air and compose myself after the emotions of the occasion.

We spent the day at the beach in a little seaside town called Viareggio. Last time I had been was New Year's Eve 2019, when, of course, I was hammered. We spent the evening strolling from bar to bar, chasing a New Year high. How things had changed. The weather was cloudy, but warm enough to relax on the beach, and Danny and Jimi read and listened to music. I lay there thinking about the last twelve months, trying to hide the tears behind my sunglasses. As the day wore on, I plucked up the courage to talk to Jimi about my guilt at being preoccupied with drinking in his teenage years.

'Were you embarrassed by me?' I asked.

'What are you on about, Mam?'

I told him I wished I could go back and change the past and how ashamed I was.

'You deserve the world, Jimi. I tried, but I know I let you down.'

The words burned into me as I admitted my failings out loud. But Jimi's forehead crumpled and he seemed confused.

'I don't remember it like that at all,' he insisted. 'I never saw you as a drunk. I didn't think you were any different to the other kids' mums who liked a glass of wine. I had a happy childhood.'

OK, we had arguments, he said, but didn't all teenagers argue with their parents? He couldn't believe I thought that way.

Now it was me who was confused and shocked. How could I have got it so wrong? I pulled Jimi towards me and hugged him to within an inch of his life. I must be driving these two mad with all my emotions today, I thought. I wished I had been brave enough to talk to Jimi sooner. Instead, I had spent years chastising myself and churning my insides up with worry. Jimi said he never thought I had a drink problem, but if I believed I did, then I had done the right thing and he was proud of me. As a family, we needed to be more open to talking to each other. And I had to address my lack of self-confidence and self-esteem. I had been my own worst enemy.

I wasn't planning to post on Facebook. I had kept my recovery private, only posting on Instagram. It was Jimi who said I should. He reminded me how hard I had worked and said I shouldn't be ashamed. If I shared my story, he said, it might help someone else. Somebody might need to see my example to change their own lives. When did this kid get so grown up? He never stopped surprising me. That was all the encouragement I needed. Jimi was a special kid and I had somehow managed to do a good job of bringing him up. His opinion mattered more than anyone else's to me. I knew he wasn't ashamed if the entire world knew about me. So I did it. I chose that photograph of me holding my cardboard one-year sign in front of the Leaning Tower of Pisa. My message received an overwhelming response, with hundreds of messages of support. The perfect way to round off my sobererversary. My news was out there now. Everyone knew now, and it felt good. It wasn't such a big deal after all.

I had experienced the most challenging year of my life and I was overcome with emotion. I never thought I would make it this far—and neither did a few others—but I did it. Despite the falling out with my parents at the start, I still made it through. I hadn't realised how strong I was. But looking back, I had always been strong. So many of us never praise ourselves. We're too busy. We need to find the time to nurture what we have and build on it.

My journey had been traumatic and pushed me further than I thought I could go. I'd faced agonising decisions, learnt ugly truths and saw myself for what I was, a hopeless drunk with no direction, overtaken by addiction. But it had also been the most rewarding year of my life. Once the layers of addiction peeled away, I learnt to love myself again. I realised I am a good person and deserve a happy life. I am a force to be reckoned with. If only I had known that years ago. I thought drinking would always be a part of me. It was who I was. But it wasn't. I was so much more than the woman who could down fifteen pints and keep up with the lads. I'd been sleepwalking for most of my life so far. But now I was wide awake. If I wanted something, I was going to make it happen. I would work hard and educate myself until I achieved my goals. I had never felt so alive, motivated and present. I had gone from being directionless to a sober superhero. Sobriety was now my superpower. I felt I could do anything now. I had the power in my own hands. It had always been there. I felt better than ever before and I knew I would grow and get better. Was it hard? Yes, of course. The hardest thing I had ever done, a twisting, tormented journey of self-discovery. But it was worth it. It was beautiful, magical and salubrious. I was finding the person I thought I had lost. It was, quite simply, life changing. Everything was better, like I was seeing the world for the first time. Brand new. Mornings felt like the start of something special, a day full of new opportunities. The sun seemed to shine brighter. My world was now a positive one. I was balanced and grounded and had grown as a person. I appreciated life more. Taking in a view of the sea, with the sun shimmering on the water, was a treat for the senses, a mystical wonder. A nice cup of tea had become my new glass of champagne. Happiness found me every day. Being around nature made me feel like I had won the lottery. This was my new world, my better world, the best version of me. I felt sorry for my old self, trapped in an endless cycle of addiction. I wished I had got sober earlier, but I couldn't regret the choices I had made. Everything that had happened to me had shaped who I now was, for better or for worse. I needed to experience it all. I had to hit rock bottom to build myself back up. Would I go back and do it again? No way. My life was too precious to me now.

Epilogue

It was November 8th 2023. The leaves had turned brown and fallen, but the sun was shining and beamed through the window. I sat on the edge of the bed, staring into the mirror. Emotions were high, a mixture of gut-churning nerves and excitement. A sense of looking down on myself and the moment not feeling quite real, but I knew it was. It didn't get any more real than this. I touched up my makeup, carefully adding soft pink lipstick, my hair curled and held up with a diamante clasp. I looked over at the white strappy dress hung on the back of the door and I smiled. I was over two years sober, and I was marrying my best friend.

We were under a pagoda at Octopus Cove in Crete. I was gazing out to sea, the sun shimmering on the gentle waves. I closed my eyes and breathed it in. It was a moment of genuine joy and clarity. I was the luckiest lady in the world. My life couldn't get any better. I had my Danny, my wonderful son Jimi, my family and friends and, most importantly, my sobriety. I had finally reached the top of my recovery mountain and I was enjoying the well-earned views. I felt a tap from behind and turned to find Danny on one knee.

'Lisa Jane,' he said. 'Will you marry me?'

I was so overcome with emotion that I forgot to say yes. As he stood up to hold me, he had to ask me again for my answer. It was an abso-bloody-loutly yes! I was in such shock. We had been together for ten years and I thought the proposal ship had sailed. We were happy as we were. This was the perfect cherry on top of our cake.

Early in the morning, we set off for Gretna Green, just over the Scottish border. We decided it would be just the two of us. We wanted our ceremony to be intimate and precious, with our only focus only on each other. Danny had left me in the hotel room to finish getting ready before making his way to the venue. I had an overwhelming feeling of being whole, a sense of belonging. I no longer felt I wasn't good enough. I now understood I was Danny's everything. He had stuck by me through my darkest days and loved me and all my flaws.

I slipped my dress on and took one last glance in the mirror. 'Look at you, Lisa Peacock,' I said out loud, grinning. I felt so proud of myself. Even I had to admit I looked amazing, and I giggled as I performed a little twirl, my sequins glittering in the sunlight. Then I caught myself. *Stop messing about. You have a wedding to get to.* I grabbed my leather jacket and bouquet and raced to meet my man at the Anvil.

Remember my dream of working with people in their most vulnerable hour, and how it would be a gift for me to support them? Well, that dream came true, too. I made sure it did. After much toing and froing and thinking I wasn't good enough, I put those old, negative thoughts and self-doubts through the shredder. They don't belong to me now. I applied to our local council to work with a recovery service. As I write this, I'm sitting in my car outside a council building, where I have an appointment to collect my ID badge and laptop. Because today, my sweets, I start my new role as an alcohol caseworker. When I started this whole recovery journey, people told me I wouldn't. Some said I couldn't. A few even laughed and said I shouldn't. Well, I've got news for them all.

I just did.

One last thing. If you can access a device, Google, Alexa, Spotify or YouTube, play Primal Scream's *Moving on Up* and think of me because that's how I feel. Elated. And my light shines on.

Don't die before you're dead

If you think you might have a problem with alcohol, please tell someone. You deserve better. Help is out there. You don't have to suffer any more. It's a tough ride and you will face dark days, but like all storms, they will eventually pass, and then you will see the rainbow. Don't die long before your life is over. I was not living, merely existing. Now I have found a better way to live.

Thank you for reading my story. Writing this book has helped me more than I can say. There is so much to be said for writing for wellness. Some things are better not shared, even with friends or family. Typing up my notes was like therapy, as I relived and reflected on my experiences. I see life so much more clearly now. Detox was a traumatic experience and reading about it again has helped me take it all in and appreciate my own strength.

I hope this book helps someone. You are not alone. You are not any less important than anyone else. You matter just as much as the person beside you and deserve to be happy.

***

And finally, a special request from me. If you enjoyed reading this book, please consider leaving a short review or even just a rating on Amazon. It only takes a few moments and will make all the difference in making sure others find out about the book and hopefully helps them in their recovery.

You can leave your review here: https://mybook.to/nodrinkforme

Thank you!

Acknowledgements

I would like to thank CGL and Recovery Connections for all the recovery support you gave me. You guys do an amazing job and are a value to the community.

Thank you Helen Aitchison for making me believe I can write a book. She told me I had a story to tell and people would listen.

A huge thank you to Michael McGeary, for helping me make it happen, for correcting my never-ending spelling and grammar mistakes and being on WhatsApp call 24/7!

Many thanks to my friends for many years of support, for never judging me and for accepting the new Lisa.

Thanks to my crazy family, who are one tent short of a circus, for getting me through life with laughter. Don't ever change.

A heartfelt thank you to my husband, Danny, for always believing in me and forever pushing me forward. I will never forget what you have done for me.

And lastly, a thank you to my wonderful son, Jimi, for never doubting me. A constant reminder and driving force to keep going. For not asking why and just simply understanding. You are my greatest achievement.

Printed in Dunstable, United Kingdom